Guide for the
College Bound

Guide for the College Bound

Everything You Need to Know

Larry Linamen, Ed. D.

Fleming H. Revell
A Division of Baker Book House
Grand Rapids, Michigan 49516

Published by Fleming H. Revell
a division of Baker Book House Company
P.O. Box 6287, Grand Rapids, MI 49516–6287

Printed in the United States of America

Library of Congress Cataloging-in-Publication Data

Linamen, Larry, 1954–
    Guide for the college bound : everything you need to know / Larry Linamen.
        p.   cm.
    Includes bibliographical references.
    ISBN 0-8007-5670-3 (pbk.)
    1. College choice—United States. 2. Church colleges—United States.
3. Universities and colleges—United States—Admission. 4. College student orientation—United States. I. Title
LB2350.5.L55   1998
378.1'61—dc21   98-23848

For current information about all releases from Baker Book House, visit our web site:
http://www.bakerbooks.com

This book is dedicated to my parents, Harold and Maxine Linamen, professors who gave their lives to Christian education. My mother taught at Anderson University until one week prior to her death. Toward the end of her teaching career you could find her carrying an oxygen tank to class or lying on the classroom floor between lectures to gain the strength for one more class. Mom, you taught me how to care for students to the end. Hundreds of students will never forget the meals you prepared for them every Saturday night for a lifetime. Your dinner rolls are remembered by students worldwide. I just hope we all have a chance to enjoy them together in heaven some day.

And to Dad, your thirty-eight years of service to Anderson University was a consistent beacon of light for generations of students and faculty. You taught me Christian scholarship, although we never discussed your books or academic accomplishments. I will never forget the year I tried to fill your shoes as a professor while you were serving as a short-term missionary in Africa. I learned from your lecture notes but I just couldn't cover it like you did. I realize now the difference was that you not only taught it, you lived it.

Several times in writing this book, I realized that these ideas were not mine, but yours. So it is only fitting that this book be dedicated to you, my parents. I love you dearly and dedicate this book to you as the scribe of your work.

Contents

Acknowledgments

The inspiration and support for this book came from several sources. For over fifteen years I have watched my wife, Karen, write books. I admired her gift as a "wordsmith" and believed she would be our only family author. But she had other plans! While I was talking one day about why someone needed to write a book on how to choose a college, she was quietly taking notes. The next thing I knew, she had shared some of these ideas with others. Karen, thank you for your love and for sharing your profession with me. You will always be the real author in our family. I also want to acknowledge my daughters, Kacie and Kaitlyn, who gave up evenings and weekends so that this book would become a reality.

Linda Holland, thank you for taking the time to help me see how I could complete this book. I must also thank the faculty and administration at Anderson, Biola, Ball State, and Dallas Baptist Universities for providing me with such a rich educational training ground.

Finally, I acknowledge our Creator for the privilege of serving him in the arena of higher education, and now for the privilege of serving him through the written word.

1

Eenie, Meenie, Miney, Moe

Making That Wise Decision

Writing from my hotel room in Taiwan, I am reminded how blessed we are in America to have such an abundance of opportunities to earn a college degree. As a vice president for a midsized private college, I frequently come across students who recognize the value of education, but few more than those I met today. While here I will be making final arrangements for Taiwanese high school teachers to come to America to pursue graduate studies at the university where I am employed. Many of these teachers will leave friends, a spouse, even young children—in fact everything they know and love—to fly around the globe to have the opportunity to finish their education.

Perhaps these Taiwanese teachers have the right idea, seeking the world over for the right education. After all, outside of the purchase of a home, a college education may well be the single most expensive investment that they—and you and I as well—

will ever make. Unfortunately too often we approach the significant decision of where to attend college with less attention, research, and forethought than we expend on choosing the family pet!

Pick a School, Any School

I have been involved in higher education for more than twenty years, beginning as a student, then faculty member, then department chairperson, then dean, and now I am serving as provost and vice president of Dallas Baptist University in—you guessed it—Dallas, Texas. The point is that during these many years, I have had the privilege of getting to know literally thousands of students. One of the questions I always like to ask them is how they decided to attend one school over all the others. You would probably be surprised at some of the tales I have heard!

Take Barbara, for example. A young woman from the Deep South, she got off the bus to find herself at a liberal arts university just outside Santa Barbara, California. From her window in the residence hall she watched students engaging in unfamiliar behavior: wearing flip-flops to class, driving expensive cars, carrying surfboards, and talking "valley talk." She was dismayed to discover that the windows to her room had no screens, and instead of the summer thunderstorms she was used to, there was constant sunshine.

While some might consider this environment heaven, Barbara was in shock—culture shock. Ready to pack her bags for home after only two days, Barbara stopped by to say good-bye to the only person she knew, a college recruiter. The concerned recruiter tried to help Barbara with her problem and after several minutes of conversation asked this key question: "So how is it that you decided to come to our university in the first place?"

Barbara replied, "I opened up a book about colleges and started down the list. When I came across this college, the book said it was in Santa Barbara. I thought to myself, *This is a sign from God!*

My name is Barbara and the city name was Barbara, so I packed up and came out to school."

Before you begin to criticize Barbara's decision-making, you should take a moment and ask yourself what criteria you are using to make your college choice. Is it possible that your method is no better than Barbara's?

Here are the ten most common comments I have heard when I've asked students why they chose a particular college or university. These responses have prompted me to write this book. I call them admissions traps.

Linamen's Top Ten Admissions Traps

1. *"The admissions counselor sure was a 'babe' (or a 'hunk'). I'll go wherever she (or he) is."*

So she looked that good! You say he was friendly? Admissions counselors are supposed to be! That's their job. My experience is that there are great-looking people—and some who look like they came from another planet—on every campus. Look for a school with the educational criteria that are important to you, and odds are you will meet people there with whom you have something in common. Remember, those admissions counselors are just a mirage in the desert preying on thirsty potential students. They can be extremely helpful but they are not what you are purchasing with your tuition dollars.

2. *"That video they sent showed major surf and sand. I bet they hold classes on the beach at this school."*

Just keeping reminding yourself that the video is only an advertisement. Yes, these are real people, but they don't surf, raft race, watch movies, act in plays, do chemistry experiments, perform a recital, and catch a nap in a gorgeous spot every day as the video portrays. It fact, the scenes may be from a field trip far removed from the actual campus setting. These videos are worth seeing, but remember, there are a lot of things missing from them. For example, how many prefabricated, temporary buildings have you seen on a university video? My experience is that almost every school has some type of trailer, old army hut, or "temporary building" that seems to mysteriously disappear when the video producers come to campus. Funny how that happens!

3. *"I didn't really want to go here but my boyfriend (girlfriend) goes here."*

Love is blind! I can't say I blame you on this one but I think you should know that some of the most heartbreaking situations I have seen involve students who have just broken up with a boyfriend or girlfriend. If this is the only reason you choose a school, it may be a very long semester. I know that those of you who are lovesick may ignore me, but mark my words, you won't regret attending the school that is best suited to your educational needs, regardless of where your honey decides to pursue a degree.

4. *"They have a great football team; it must be a great school."*

Studies have shown that people tend to evaluate the quality of a university's academic program by the quality of its sports program. There is no correlation between the two. We all like winners, but for most of us, our college team record has very little to do with our success in life. On a visit to the Northwest, I had the opportunity to attend a home game of a major university with a top-ranked football team. I was excited to see this powerhouse football program in action until the cheerleaders got up to give their first cheer. Instead of using the correct words to the cheer, the students chanted in unison a perverted version filled with curse words. After the game, I expected students to be excited about the victory. Instead, they seemed more impressed with the fact that, during the game, television coverage was interrupted by drunken students who climbed onto a platform and urinated on the TV camera crew. I wonder how many people who recommend this school to students know the whole story.

5. *"The concert they had for admissions weekend was awesome. I bet they have events like this every weekend."*

Preview weekends for new students are great but they may give the impression that college is like a summer camp or continuous music festival. While most campuses provide a large number of activities outside of classes, don't expect admissions weekends to represent typical days. Again, don't pick the school because you like an event; instead, use your time on campus to evaluate the whole institution.

6. *"I think I will go to this university because the counselor says everyone has heard of it and the bumper sticker will look great on my car."*

While there is some value in a school's reputation, many schools are known simply because they have twenty thousand students. Does mere size indicate quality? Not necessarily. I am always amazed how shallow these good reputations are that we hear so much about. Next time someone tells you University X is a good school, ask why. Most people, unless they are recent graduates of the institution, can tell you very few actual facts about the school. Instead, they usually know someone who went there and too often affiliate their fondness or respect for this alumni friend with the school's reputation. I have also found that a college's reputation usually lags about three to ten years behind what is currently happening on the campus. Often a few phone calls and some digging around will reveal, for example, that the faculty members who helped develop a certain fine department are now teaching at another university.

7. *"A Christian school would be great, but I can't afford one."*

The vast majority of students who attend Christian schools today receive financial aid of some kind. Before you decide that you can't attend the school of your choice, take the time to fill out the necessary forms and ask for information about scholarships in addition to the ones that are openly advertised. Then apply for them early.

8. *"I didn't check it out, but they tell me this university is rated in the top ten."*

Be very careful with this one. Before you put any weight in ratings, remember to analyze the criteria used to evaluate the schools. Some evaluations I have seen specifically exclude church-related schools from their rating system. Without knowing this, you may come to the conclusion that Christian schools simply are not on a par with their secular counterparts. This, of course, is not an accurate assessment.

Let me give you one more example. One well-known top-ten list, published annually by *U.S. News and World Report,* bases 25 percent of its ratings on the opinions of 2,730 university administrators (single greatest component in the ranking process).[1] When I participated in this evaluation process, I must confess that I had not heard of many of the schools in some states that were almost one thousand miles away. Since there is no description of the institutions on the survey form and literally hundreds to evaluate, there is little chance that a busy administrator will do any serious research to become familiar with these unknown schools. It doesn't take a lot of brainpower to figure out that good regional universities are at a serious disadvantage in this process when compared with nationally known sports schools. If a school isn't known outside its area, it doesn't matter how good its programs are, it will not receive enough votes to qualify for a good rating.

In fact, there are enough people disturbed about this rating system that there is a nationwide movement of students—many of them at prestigious universities—hoping to reform the method magazines use to rate higher education. This organization, called Forget U.S. News Coalition (FUNC), includes students from schools like University of Oklahoma, Rice University, University of Houston, University of Michigan, University of California at Berkeley, and Massachusetts Institute of Technology. These students question how ratings can vary so much from year to year when the schools involved have made few changes. "Universities are slow-moving machines, and what can they do that's so wrong that would cause them to drop several places?" questions Jeff Tsai from the University of Texas at Austin.[2]

Be careful of choosing a college based on these rating systems. Listen to the students from across the country.

9. *"I hear Christian universities don't have such good academic programs."*

There are Christian schools that are not regionally accredited (see discussion in chapter 9) and that do not have good academic programs, just as there are secular schools with the same problems. The good news is that there are also many strong Christian colleges and universities that, among them, offer hundreds of majors. In the following chapters I'll present information to help you evaluate the academics and overall quality of schools that you may be considering.

10. *"I didn't know where to go, and this was the first school to respond to my application."*

This could mean that the school has a very efficient applicant-response system, or it could mean the school is desperate for students. While it is great to get that first letter of acceptance, especially if it is from your school of choice, it doesn't hurt to apply to several institutions and then wait to see what options you are given. Think of this as shopping. Most people do not buy the first car someone is willing to sell them, so why buy the first education that comes along?

Purpose of This Book

If some of those traps sound familiar, you're reading the right book. The purpose of this book is to help you steer clear of those traps rather than fall into them. Future chapters will alert you to the nature of colleges today and arm you with tools to help you evaluate very specifically any given university and how well it meets a Christian student's needs and expectations. There will always be challenging experiences and adjustments in college, but after reading this book, families should be able to feel confident that they are investing in the right education. The good news is there are many academically strong Christian colleges and universities that do not take faith lightly, and at most public institutions, there are active Christian student groups. Finding the options that best meet your needs is the key.

2

We're Not in Kansas Anymore, Toto!

Colleges and Universities Today

Did your dad ever tell you about the time he and his roommates put shoe polish on the black toilet seats in the residence hall? Did your mom tell you how she and a group of students toilet-papered the president's home? Did Grandpa tell you that he fell in love with the May queen (you know her today as Grandma) the first time he spotted her at the campus malt shop?

Many families have fun memories of college days, often some of their best memories. If this is true in your family, you may have relatives who are encouraging you to attend the same school they did, and they may be right. Perhaps the school they attended will be a great place for you to study as well. Sometimes, however, these schools have changed over the years and evolved into very different institutions. From gay rights and coed dorms to religion and technology, the atmosphere on college campuses is changing. Here is a brief look at some of the ways universities today are different than they were twenty years ago.

Sexual Orientation

Under the label of diversity, disturbing changes are taking place on many campuses today with regard to gay rights and other issues related to sexual orientation. Let me give you just one example:

> A few years ago reportedly Jerome Penn entered the University of Michigan to discover that his roommate had covered the walls with posters and photographs of nude men. Jerome's roommate shared with him that he was an active homosexual and that he intended to bring sexual partners to their dorm room. When Penn went to housing to be reassigned to another room, the housing office was "outraged" at his request. "They asked me what was wrong with me, what my problem was. I said that I had a religious and moral objection to homosexual conduct. They were surprised; they couldn't believe it. Finally they agreed to assign me to another room, but they warned me that if I told anyone of the reason, I would face university charges of discrimination on the basis of sexual orientation."[1]

Alarmingly, Penn's religious rights were expected to take a backseat to rights associated with sexual orientation, a situation that would be unheard of even one generation ago. Is this an isolated, one-of-a-kind situation? I wish I could say that it was.

Unfortunately, some of the schools that have changed the most in this area are schools that started out as Christian universities. Take the case of Yale University, an institution with an outstanding reputation. Indeed, in 1937 Yale President Charles Seymour in his inaugural speech made the following profound statement regarding the integration of Christianity and education:

> I call on all members of the faculty, as members of a thinking body, freely to recognize the tremendous validity and power of the teachings of Christ in our life-and-death struggle against selfish materialism. If we lose that struggle, judging from present events abroad, scholarship as well as religion will disappear. . . . the maintenance and upbuilding of the Christian religion is a vital part of the university life.[2]

Today there may be a few people who would argue that Yale remains a Christian university. Yet many others seriously question if the principles found in Charles Seymour's inaugural speech are still central to the institution today.

For example, by 1987—just fifty years after Seymour's inaugural speech—the changes in Yale were so apparent that the *Wall Street Journal* ran an article titled "Lipsticks and Lords: Yale's New Look" by Julie Iovine, which talked about the large gay population on campus and the gay reputation Yale had developed. Iovine wrote:

> Yale has no less than five gay and lesbian groups, including one just for Chicano lesbians. More than a thousand students attend Yale's annual gay and lesbian ball and gay activist Sara Cohen asks, "What's wrong with a little bestiality?" Concerned that this flagrancy would upset alumni donors, President Benno Schmidt of Yale promptly sent a letter to two thousand volunteer fund-raisers denying that Yale was a "gay school" and concluding, "If I thought there were any truth to the article, I would be concerned too." Schmidt's statement caused an eruption at the university. A graduate student announced that he was canceling his course in homosexual rights. Gay activist groups besieged Schmidt and demanded to know: what was wrong with 25 or even 70 percent of Yale students being homosexual? What was wrong with Yale being a gay school? Somewhat chagrined, Schmidt responded that no, there wouldn't be anything wrong with that, but Yale needed to have a proportionate number of heterosexuals too—for the sake of diversity.[3]

A recent review of the "Freshperson Issue" via the Yale home page revealed a series of articles written to new freshmen prospects in the way of orientation. One such article titled "Boola-Boolas Can Still Make Whoopee—There's Nothing Academic about Campus Sex" by Julie Hirschfeld provided a list of out-of-the-way Yale campus locations in which to have sex. Written to readers in the format of an informative article, descriptions of library stacks and public campus towers are given as recommended clandestine spots for student sexual encounters.

It appears that Yale has wandered far from where it was when Grandpa was college age!

If you think that somehow Yale is the exception, take Dartmouth, a school originally founded as a missionary outreach to the Indians and another school of outstanding academic reputation. In more recent years, during registration Dartmouth students were issued a "safer sex kit," which was described as being "for everyone—homosexual, bisexual, and heterosexual." While the enclosed documents did mention abstinence as an option, recipients of the kit were encouraged to be creative and imaginative with the devices contained inside. The kit goes further to state that "sex is too important a personal decision" for someone else to decide, but friends might be consulted along the way. Parents are recommended only at the point when a relationship falls apart, to help pick up the pieces.[4]

Coed Housing

Another change in direction on many college campuses is in the area of coed housing. An extensive questionnaire mailed to student affairs officers on seventy-five college campuses revealed the following statistics about the dramatic increase in coed dorms on campuses:

Male/Female Housing on College Campuses[5]

	1970	1980	1990
Separate Men's and Women's Housing	77%	23%	10%
Alternate Floors	19%	41%	40%
Alternate Rooms or Suites	3%	36%	50%

Notice that in 1970 nearly eight out of ten college campuses provided separate housing for men and women. Two decades later, the numbers had flip-flopped and then some, with nine out of ten schools providing some form of coed housing. While this survey included very few Christian campuses, it is clear that students on most secular campuses will encounter a residence hall life that their parents did not experience. Now, instead of the occasional overnight visitor hiding from watchful residence assistants, there are new issues to face. Among other things, residence directors now deal with male and female students who have swapped roommates. If one of the couples involved in the swap breaks up, a very complex housing problem is created. One anthropologist, Michael Moffatt, observed coed dorms at Rutgers and reported that men and women did not ordinarily walk the halls naked; even so, the changes in campus housing have dramatically impacted campus life.[6]

Don't Be Fooled by a Name

As we have seen, many schools no longer hold to standards that were important to their founders. Some schools retain a name that no longer reflects the standards of the campus.

A university in the Southwest, for example, recently made a point to inform new faculty that although the university had a religious name, faculty were not expected to teach from a Christian perspective. Sadly, some university names now represent only the ghosts of the forefathers, and their mission statements are in place more to please alumni and donors than to serve as serious guideposts for teaching. Without some research well beyond the catalog and recruiting videos, it is often difficult to tell the true nature of the institution. The good news is that by the time you finish reading this book, you will be well versed in ways to discern the true character of virtually any college or university.

The New Technology

Not all trends in education are negative. Imagine this scenario, which illustrates a few of our advancements in technology: It's 7 A.M. and you just woke up to the sound of your favorite song, courtesy of digital music on your computer. Before you can put on your shorts, your computer has already turned on the toaster, cooked your favorite breakfast, and done your homework.

All right, so I'm stretching it a little, but I can tell you that college assignments today don't necessarily have to resemble the ones your parents were asked to complete. Instead of spending hours in front of a card catalog and wandering hopelessly through library stacks only to find the book you need has already been checked out, it is now possible in some schools to accomplish library research online, on your home computer at any hour of the night or day. If this is not enough, you may decide to "surf" the Internet for more research sources and find yourself wandering electronically through a library in Israel or some other part of the globe.

Additionally, with the help of two-way interactive video, you may now take a course with classmates who are in Pennsylvania or Hong Kong and with guest speakers coming live to you from a different state each week. There are now individual computer workstations where students may simply log into class via modem and participate in the class discussion.

In chapter 4 I take a closer look at technology and education, giving suggestions on how you can search for the college best suited to your needs by using Internet home pages. In fact, technology has changed so much in the past generation that you can now complete your whole college degree on the Internet at schools like the University of Phoenix (see chapter 15). Tell me life hasn't changed! (I wonder how they do PE by computer. Maybe you can take a class in cyber-bowling.)

I mention these changes on college campuses, not to scare or overwhelm you, but simply to better prepare you for the choices you need to make. I really want to encourage you to take seriously the task of choosing the right college. It is a responsibility but it is also a tremendous opportunity and privilege. In this process, I can't overstate the importance of researching the schools you are considering. Visit the campuses. Talk to professors, alumni, and current students. You can even subscribe in advance to the student newspaper! It may sound like a lot of work, but let me assure you it can also be a lot of fun. And best of all, you're not walking this path alone. My goal in writing this book is to accompany you on this journey, sharing encouragement, inspiration, and practical help that only an insider can provide.

3

Can I Really Afford It?

Financial Hope for Today's Families

I was trying to figure out how in the world I was going to get into a Christian school. We had already ruled out living on campus because it was too expensive. Well, that still left us short of money. So my family and I prayed that if it was right for me to be applying to this college, God would help us through this financial situation. Two weeks later in the mail we received the packet back from the government with a letter saying I was eligible for three thousand dollars in grants. This was the "light" we were hoping for. God pulled us through, and here I am!

Laurel Vokovich

If you are concerned about how you are going to pay for college, you are not alone. The Higher Education Research Institute at UCLA found that one in three of 1996 college freshmen rated financial aid as a "very important" factor in selecting a college. The number jumped to almost seven out of ten freshmen who expressed concern when they were asked about how they would pay for their education.[1]

Unfortunately, financial aid has not kept pace with the rise in tuition costs. And to make matters worse, too many students give up seeking aid before they explore all the options.

So how are other students managing to pay for college? The following table provides a summary of 251,232 freshmen from 494 universities with regard to the sources of money for college. Let's take a look.

Sources of Revenue to Pay College Tuition for Traditional Age Freshmen Entering Fall 1996 [2]

Source	Percentage of Tuition Contributed	Source	Percentage of Tuition Contributed
Parents, relatives, or friends	76%	Other private grant	11%
Savings from summer work	50	Other college loan	9
Other savings	31	Perkins loan	9
Other college grant	29	Other loan	6
Stafford/ guaranteed loan	26	SEOG (Supplemental educational opportunity grants)	6
Part-time job off campus	25	Full-time job	4
Part-time job on campus	22	Other government sources (ROTC, GI)	3
Pell grant	20	Spouse	1
State scholarship	17	Vocational rehabilitation funds	1
College work-study	12	Other source	4

Far and away the most common funding sources are parents, relatives, and friends (76 percent). Another common source is savings from summer work (50 percent). You'll notice that loans, scholarships, and grants play a significant role as well. The point I'd like to make is that there are many options, perhaps more than you may have realized. So don't get discouraged. College isn't cheap but it's an investment worth making, and lots of other students are finding ways to make the dollars make sense—my guess is that you can too.

Let's walk through some options.

Tuition Rates

Before we delve into loans and other kinds of financial aid, let's start with something even more basic than that. Let's talk about tuition prices.

It pays to keep in mind that a high tuition doesn't always mean better education. Take the case of New York's Adelphi University. Since 1990, tuition at this school has increased roughly 60 percent. Do more tuition dollars mean better education? Let's look at some additional facts about the school: In the past ten years, student enrollment at Adelphi has dropped 30 percent, and one-third of the faculty has left the institution. If tuition dollars aren't helping student and faculty retention, what are they being used for? One clue may be found in the fact that in 1994, Adelphi paid its president, Peter Diamandopoulos, $522,000 in salary and conditional bonuses, making Diamandopoulos the second-highest-paid college president in the country.[3] Given the loss of faculty and students combined with such a high salary for the president, one must question whether the dramatic tuition increase has substantially improved the quality of education on this campus.

Other factors besides the president's salary can affect tuition rates. These include geographic location, denominational support, and the size of the university endowment.

Geographic Location

With regard to geographic location, it's interesting to note that colleges on the West Coast tend to be considerably more expensive than institutions in the South. As you can see from the following table giving the 1995–96 tuition rates of eighty-eight different Christian colleges, the average total cost per year for a private Christian college in the West is $15,666, while the average total cost in the South is $11,323. Much of the $4,343 difference between the West and South can be attributed to cost of living.

If you live in an area where college tuition is typically higher than in other parts of the country and you are willing to leave home and travel away to school—say, from California to Georgia—you may be able to cut thousands of dollars off your college bill because private Christian colleges do not raise their rate for out-of-state students as do many public universities. This geographic discount alone could be better than many scholarships. Granted, you will need to add back some expense for travel and long-distance phone calls, but it's unlikely that these expenses will make up for your savings.

On the other hand, attending a Christian college within commuting distance of your home will cut about four thousand dollars off your total bill per year if you decide to live at home rather than in a dorm. There are some definite advantages to living on campus, but often this decision becomes more of a financial decision than an educational choice. You may have to do some figuring to determine which option will save you more money: living on campus at an out-of-state school that offers cheaper tuition, or paying higher tuition at a local school that will allow you to commute to campus. Your family will need to discuss the pros and cons of each option and decide what is best for you.

Denominational Support

Another factor that can affect tuition is church affiliation. Denominations often meet 1 to 15 percent of the annual budget of schools owned by or closely aligned with the denomination. This, of course, helps reduce overall college costs. While it is always preferable to go to a school that shares your theological beliefs, most Christian schools do not change the price of tuition on the basis of your denominational persuasion. In fact, many do not require a statement of faith to attend.

Coalition for Christian Colleges and Universities Tuition Costs

School	Tuition & Fees	Room & Board	Total
WEST			
Westmont College	$16,330	$5,580	$21,910
George Fox University	$14,520	$4,640	$19,160
Seattle Pacific University	$13,680	$5,244	$18,924
Whitworth College	$13,685	$5,000	$18,685
Biola University	$13,408	$4,468	$17,876
Azusa Pacific University	$13,076	$4,200	$17,276
Southern California College	$11,126	$4,752	$15,878
The Master's College	$10,990	$4,534	$15,524
Point Loma Nazarene College	$11,020	$4,480	$15,500
Western Baptist College	$10,940	$4,550	$15,490
Fresno Pacific University	$11,430	$3,920	$15,350
Warner Pacific College	$9,642	$3,750	$13,392
California Baptist College	$8,236	$4,494	$12,730
Hope International University	$8,835	$3,584	$12,419
Northwest College	$8,415	$3,990	$12,405
Simpson College	$8,474	$3,800	$12,274
Grand Canyon University	$8,368	$3,160	$11,528
Average	**$11,304**	**$4,362**	**$15,666**
MIDWEST			
North Park University	$13,990	$4,610	$18,600
Bethel College (Minn.)	$13,180	$4,490	$17,670
Wheaton College	$13,100	$4,550	$17,650
Taylor University	$12,774	$4,220	$16,994
Northwestern College (Minn.)	$12,750	$4,080	$16,830

School	Tuition & Fees	Room & Board	Total
Greenville College	$11,750	$4,750	$16,500
Bluffton College	$11,250	$4,641	$15,891
Huntington College	$11,520	$4,340	$15,860
Calvin College	$11,655	$4,160	$15,815
Trinity Christian College	$11,250	$4,435	$15,685
Trinity International University	$11,140	$4,420	$15,560
Malone College	$10,765	$4,300	$15,065
Judson College	$10,334	$4,690	$15,024
Anderson University	$11,240	$3,750	$14,990
Northwest Nazarene College	$11,685	$3,270	$14,955
Goshen College	$10,900	$3,880	$14,780
Olivet Nazarene University	$10,166	$4,460	$14,626
Spring Arbor College	$10,386	$4,070	$14,456
Indiana Wesleyan University	$10,260	$4,042	$14,302
Northwestern College (Iowa)	$10,850	$3,250	$14,100
Dordt College	$10,800	$2,900	$13,700
Grace College	$9,506	$4,146	$13,652
Tabor College	$9,900	$3,750	$13,650
University of Sioux Falls	$10,120	$3,420	$13,540
Sterling College	$9,696	$3,784	$13,480
Mount Vernon Nazarene College	$9,390	$3,720	$13,110
Bethel College (Ind.)	$9,750	$3,100	$12,850
Bethel College (Kans.)	$9,270	$3,800	$13,070
Cornerstone College	$8,686	$4,266	$12,952
MidAmerica Nazarene College	$8,668	$4,202	$12,870
Colorado Christian University	$8,855	$3,930	$12,785
Asbury College	$9,819	$2,890	$12,709
Cedarville College	$8,004	$4,572	$12,576
Evangel College	$7,680	$3,340	$11,020
Average	**$10,620**	**$4,007**	**$14,627**

School	Tuition & Fees	Room & Board	Total
SOUTH			
LeTourneau University	$11,030	$4,630	$15,660
King College	$10,280	$3,444	$13,724
Bryan College	$9,700	$3,950	$13,650
Palm Beach Atlantic College	$9,300	$4,310	$13,610
Milligan College	$9,500	$3,440	$12,940
John Brown University	$8,308	$4,224	$12,532
Abilene Christian University	$8,520	$3,580	$12,100
Warner Southern College	$7,900	$3,816	$11,716
Trevecca Nazarene University	$7,856	$3,410	$11,266
Bartlesville Wesleyan College	$7,600	$3,600	$11,200
Belhaven College	$8,040	$3,100	$11,140
Southern Nazarene University	$7,128	$3,810	$10,938
Dallas Baptist University	$7,140	$3,250	$10,390
Southwest Baptist University	$7,708	$2,623	$10,331
Oklahoma Baptist University	$6,524	$3,270	$9,794
Union University	$7,030	$2,700	$9,730
Campbellsville University	$6,420	$3,210	$9,630
East Texas Baptist University	$6,490	$3,000	$9,490
Lee College	$5,372	$3,540	$8,912
Williams Baptist College	$4,990	$2,722	$7,712
Average	**$7,842**	**$3,481**	**$11,323**
SOUTHEAST			
Erskine College	$11,908	$4,086	$15,994
Covenant College	$10,920	$3,996	$14,916
Montreat College	$9,656	$3,752	$13,408

School	Tuition & Fees	Room & Board	Total
Southern Wesleyan University	$9,615	$3,380	$12,995
Campbell University	$8,980	$3,350	$12,330
Average	**$10,216**	**$3,713**	**$13,929**

EAST ───────────────────────────

Gordon College	$13,950	$4,440	$18,390
Eastern College	$11,750	$5,036	$16,786
Messiah College	$10,954	$5,040	$15,994
Houghton College	$11,700	$3,998	$15,698
Roberts Wesleyan College	$11,640	$4,056	$15,696
Eastern Mennonite University	$11,130	$4,200	$15,330
Geneva College	$10,784	$4,500	$15,284
Nyack College	$10,360	$4,420	$14,780
Eastern Nazarene College	$10,816	$3,750	$14,566
Average	**$11,454**	**$4,382**	**$15,836**

CANADA ─────────────────────────

Trinity Western University	$8,075	$4,990	$13,065
Redeemer College	$7,863	$4,180	$12,043
The King's University College	$4,515	$4,415	$8,930
Average	**$6,818**	**$4,528**	**$11,346**

Endowments

Some universities have developed large endowments through gifts and other sources that help keep tuition rates down. An endowment is a university savings account that earns interest. Each year the school receives interest on its money, which it can use to operate the university. Since this money is generally invested conservatively, a school may earn between 5 and 9 percent on its money in a given year. So if a school has an endowment of 50 million dollars and earns 6 percent on its money, the school would receive 3 million dollars a year to operate the school. The larger the endowment to help operate the school, the less dependent the school is on your tuition. It's as simple as that.

Private Secular Schools

Christian schools may seem terribly expensive but they are generally cheaper than their private secular counterparts. A study done by Dr. Meredith A. Whiteley concluded that the average tuition for the ninety schools in the Coalition for Christian Colleges and Universities (CCCU) was actually $2,530 below the average tuition cost of all four-year private institutions.[4]

The real tuition difference exists between private universities and state-run institutions because public institutions are subsidized by tax dollars. As long as private universities pay their own way while public institutions continue to receive significant government aid, there will be a substantial difference in the cost of tuition.

The good news, however, is that a study of debt accumulated by seniors who attended private and those who attended public colleges and universities indicates that cumulative debt is not substantially different between the two groups. The study discovered that college seniors who attended public institutions graduated from school owing an average of $12,561 in school loans. College seniors who attended private schools, on the other hand, reported being about $15,136 in debt. While the study did not take into account credit card debt or new debt incurred by parents for either

33

group, the difference in cumulative debt from federal, state, and private loans was only $2,575 between the two groups.[5]

It is encouraging to note that students in private institutions are finding sources for financial support and are graduating with no more debt than if they purchased a new car.

But wait . . . there's more good news . . .

According to Dr. David Warren, president of the National Association of Independent Colleges and Universities, the average family has a real misunderstanding of what a private education actually costs. Warren reports that the average private education today averages about $12,500 a year, but most families estimate it to be closer to $20,000. Actually, only 1.7 percent of the colleges in the United States charge tuition above $20,000 and only about one-third of the students who attend these schools pay the full tuition amount. Even at the cheaper private universities, about half the students receive some tuition aid in the form of grants and scholarships so they are not paying the full tuition amount.[6]

Watch Out for the Fees

Well, we've looked at tuition. But before we're ready to talk about financial aid, there's another category of expenses of which you need to be aware.

Recently some states have cut back the number of tax dollars being used to support public education. Since many public universities have had their tuition figures controlled by the state, they have been forced to look for new sources of revenue. One common source has been through increasing existing fees and creating new fees for other services that used to be covered in the basic tuition. As a result, you may find fees to be much higher than you had originally budgeted. The proliferation of fees in public education is another reason why the difference between the cost of a public education and a private one may be less than you originally thought.

By way of example, for students from California there is no tuition expense at UCLA. Only nonresidents pay tuition. Great news for Californians, right? But what about fees? Well, that's another matter. Here is a list of fees that UCLA charges each student.[7]

University registration fee	$ 713
Educational fee	3,086
Ackerman Student Union fee	7
USA fee	54
Wooden Recreational Center fee	33
Seismic fee for Ackerman/Kerckhoff	133
Total fees per quarter	$4,006

UCLA is very open about all fee charges when asked, but it may appear misleading to a student who is told that tuition is free and yet ends up with a four-thousand-dollar bill anyway. Particularly curious is the Seismic fee for Ackerman/Kerckhoff. Are we to assume that this is an assessment for earthquake protection for some buildings, or have two mad scientists named Ackerman and Kerckhoff found a way to add their own fees to support research on the mating habits of the Goliath beetle under various levels of seismic activity? When we asked about this fee, the people we reached were not clear on what it is. I hope someone at UCLA knows what these fees are for.

If you think UCLA fees are odd, assume for a moment you are a student at Indiana University. All full-time students pay a flat tuition charge regardless of how many credit hours they are taking. That seems simple enough. But then the fees kick in, and that's where things get confusing. First, there is a mandatory activity fee. How much is it? Well, are you taking three credit hours or more than three credit hours? Are you taking these classes in the summer or during the regular semester? If you take more than three credit hours, you also have to add a student health fee, but again the amount varies depending on whether or not it is a regular semester or another session. But if it is in the summer, the student health fee varies depending on whether it is summer I or summer II.

Now, once you have paid these fees you need to calculate your technology fee. For this one you need a chart, which shows your fee based on class standing and the number of credit hours.

Indiana University Technology Fee Chart

	3 Credit Hours or Fewer	Between 3 and 6.5 Credit Hours	6.5 Credit Hours or Above
Undergraduate	$25	$50	$100
Graduate/Professional	12	25	50
Nondegree	12	25	50

Don't ask me how you could end up with 6.5 credit hours, but nothing is simple here. Well, we're not done yet. If you decide to take a music course, there is a music fee, which varies depending on whether you are a music major, nonmusic major, or nondegree student. Oh, and of course we have to calculate this fee based on whether or not this will be a summer course.

If you choose an education course, there will be a different education fee added, depending on which course you take. By looking up your course on a chart, you can determine the fee. For example, if you take M403, you pay the education early experience fee; but if you take M470, then you must pay the education practicum fee; and then again if you take M423, you pay the education student teaching fee.

Getting confused yet? If this is not enough there are special fees for classes in film studies, ceramics, computer art, graphic design, jewelry, photography, printmaking, sculpture, textiles, billiards, bowling, fencing, golf, landscape horticulture, personal fitness, riflery, rowing, sailing, scientific driver certification (what is this?), scuba, skiing, tennis, trap and skeet, underwater science techniques, and journalism. Finally, there are more than two hundred courses with lab fees, and there are miscellaneous fees for everything from a deferment service charge to fees for placement and career planning. The fee listings in the Indiana University catalog go on for fourteen pages! Have I made my point or am I going to have to bore you with more?

I can summarize this in one sentence. When you set your budget to go to school, take fees into account, in addition to all the other costs in your financial decision.

Despite the high cost of a college education, statistics still indicate that college is a worthwhile investment. During an average lifetime of work (forty years), a man with a bachelor's degree earns $700,000 more than someone who graduated only from high school. A woman with a bachelor's degree will earn on average about $400,000 more than her counterparts with high school degrees. "The only thing more expensive than going to college is *not* going to college," comments Tom Mortenson, the director of the Center for Study of Opportunities in Higher Education.[8]

Scholarships, Grants, and Loans

Let's assume for a moment that you have considered geography, tuition, dorm living versus commuting, and even fees . . . and you're still a long way off from having the money you need to get your education. The good news is that there are numerous grants and loans available from legitimate institutions, including strong Christian universities that give aid to worthy students. The first important point to understand about tuition is that very few students pay the full sticker price of a college education. At some universities, for example, the majority of their students pay only about 50 percent of the bill up front with the remainder coming from scholarships, grants, and loans.

Here are some tips to help you in your search to come up with additional financial resources.

1. *Assess your skills.* First of all, do a self-assessment of your own skills. Are you a singer or have you been involved in a debate team? Many Christian and secular schools give scholarships to students with these talents. It is not just the athletes for whom scholarships are available. The challenge is finding schools that offer this type of aid. One place to begin would be a review of Internet sites (see chapter 4 for more information on Internet resources) to determine where majors and programs exist around

the country. Keep in mind that if you are a borderline candidate at a school, your chances of getting aid are not as good as they are if you apply to a school where you fit into the mainstream of students applying.

2. *File for financial aid.* Filing for financial aid is a rather complex and labor-intensive process. Different schools have different processes, but here are some of the basics.

A good place to start is the Free Application for Federal Student Aid (FAFSA). This is a financial aid form provided by the government for the purpose of determining—based on your family income, debts, and assets—whether or not you are eligible for federal grants. The form has more than one hundred blanks, with much of the information requested related to your family's income and assets. I would suggest you do a rough draft in pencil before putting the information on your final form. If you encounter questions you don't understand or need a copy of the form, contact the financial aid office of the school to which you are applying or ask your high school guidance counselor. You can also obtain the form by calling 1-800-4FED-AID.

About three to five weeks after you send in the completed form, you will receive back a Student Aid Report (SAR), which repeats back to you much of the information you submitted combined with your expected family contribution (EFC). The expected family contribution is the amount of money that, based on your family income, the government believes your family should be able to come up with to pay for your college education.

A good scenario would be to get a report back from your school of application saying that your full need has been met. In other words, after your expected family contribution has been made from your own pocket, the rest of the college tuition has been covered by scholarships, grants, and loans. However, increasingly there are cases where colleges cannot make up the full unmet need. The difference between what the school can offer in various forms of aid and what you still need to pay is called the "need gap."

For example, let's assume you wish to go to VT Public University (don't go looking for this school because it doesn't exist), and the cost is $5,600 for tuition, room, and board. After sending in your FAFSA paperwork, you receive back an EFC amount of $3,000. The college has put a package together for you of $2,300 in aid. How much are you going to have to come up with in order to go to school at VT Public University? Here are the calculations:

Tuition, room, and board charge	$ 5,600
Less expected family contribution	–3,000
Less aid package	–2,300
Equals need gap	$ 300

Since your family must come up with the expected family contribution and would also have to pay the need gap, the total amount you would pay for this year is $3,300. Well, sort of . . . want the rest of the news? Often part of the aid package you receive from a college will be a loan. While you don't have to pay anything back on it or any interest while you are in school, after you get out of school, the payments will start.

Does all of this mean that if a private Christian university costs $11,000 in tuition, room, and board, you will not be able to afford it? Not necessarily, because the aid package may be more substantial from this school. Suppose the aid package at VT Christian University (again, don't go out looking for this school) was $6,000. Here are the numbers:

Tuition, room, and board charge	$ 11,000
Less expected family contribution	–3,000
Less aid package	–6,000
Equals need gap	$ 2,000

To go to VT Christian University you would pay $5,000 for the year (EFC $3,000 + gap $2,000) as compared to $3,300 (EFC $3,000 + gap $300) at VT Public University. In this case the difference in your payment would be only $1,700, even though the difference in tuition is actually $5,400. All of this is to say, don't give up on a private Christian university you want to attend until you have gone through the financial aid process and have seen the bottom line.

I received a full scholarship to two state schools, but I really wanted to go to a Christian school, where I was not receiving enough financial aid. I had signed up for state school registration and had resigned myself to being a freshman there. To come to a Christian school I needed another grant and another scholarship. My admissions counselor worked hard and at 5 p.m. the night before registration, I found out that I got the scholarship, grant, plus a loan. It was really a miracle.

Carleigh Kazee

3. *Do your own scholarship search.* There is nothing that says you must accept only the aid options your school can provide. Anything else you can come up with just makes it that much easier. Every year some aid goes unclaimed because no one who fits the scholarship criteria applied. There are services that will research options for a fee, but the best options I have found are free on the Internet.

For example, an excellent source titled Fast Web has more than ten million reported sources for funding and reports that they are adding approximately twelve hundred new awards to their database per day. Their Web site address is http://www.fastweb.com. In a six-step process that takes no more than thirty minutes you can have a listing of potential funding sources to which you can apply based on your unique situation. Most of these will be potential additional sources of funding beyond that provided through your university.

If you don't have a computer or would rather work with a paid scholarship research service, be careful how you select the provider. Unfortunately, scam artists exist who will guarantee scholarship results (for a fee of ten or twenty dollars) and then cannot deliver on their promises. One warning sign is if the service asks you to provide any money up front. They may tell you that the money is needed for application fees, yet application fees are rarely required by scholarship and grant foundations.

Another warning sign should be any company claiming huge success rates. According to the Web site "Guarantees of High

Response Rate or Your Money Back: The Scholarship Scam Alert" (an excellent free source on scams and how to avoid them) at http://www.finaid.org, less than 1 percent of those using scholarship search services actually receive an award, so any claim of a 95 percent success rate or your money back is highly suspect.

4. *Get a job.* A very common option chosen by many of today's students to help pay the bills is to hold down a job while in college. *Prospectus* newsletter (December 1996) reports that almost two out of every students (62 percent) are employed during the school year. Many of these students are adults who work full time. In their own survey, the Higher Education Research Institute discovered that 41 percent of traditional-age freshmen expected to work to pay for school.[9]

Whatever your age group, working your way through school is a viable option. The average traditional student earns $129 a week while in college. This may help you to know how much you can reasonably expect to contribute toward your education while going to school.

One caution here. While it is obviously possible to earn more than $129 a week, you should be careful not to work too much during your college years. While some work can actually put discipline into your schedule, provide money for your pocket, and improve your educational experience, the decision to work full time while in school should be seriously evaluated before classes begin.

Normally I would not suggest going into debt, but in the case of education it often makes financial sense to take out a low-interest government loan. Studies show that traditional students who go straight through school, get a job in their field, and then pay off their educational loans come out financially ahead of students who choose a pay-as-you-go plan, making only a little above minimum wage throughout an extended college career.

Doing What It Takes

I once heard the story of a young man who volunteered to play the piano for a church service. When the day came, he calmly sat down at the keyboard in front of the congregation. As he began to play, instead of fine music, all that came out was noise. Everyone sat in shock until soon the young man left the building in disgrace. It turned out that this student had never learned to play the piano. He believed that if he just asked God for the gift of music, it would be given to him. In light of his lack of preparation, his failure comes as no surprise. In fact, it was virtually guaranteed!

The same is true of the financial aid search. All too often I hear wanna-be students excuse their lack of preparation by saying, "If God wants me to go to school, he'll provide the money." Other students appear on campus at the eleventh hour and ask if they can get financial aid—before classes start next week!

The truth is that it takes work to get financial aid just as it takes work to learn to play the piano. The information given in this chapter can go a long way toward making your dream possible, but don't make the mistake of saying "If God wants me to go, he will provide the way" as an excuse for not doing the work you need to do.

The good news is that most of you reading this can go to a private Christian college if you really want to. Here are some suggestions:

- Start early and make application for aid to as many sources as possible. A good rule of thumb is to begin applying eighteen months before you plan to begin school.
- Have a teacher or parent edit and read your application for any errors that could eliminate you as a recipient of aid in a competitive market.
- Be prepared for the possibility that you will have some education loans to pay back when you graduate. Better to graduate owing some money than to not graduate at all. Look at your education as an investment in the future rather than a cost in the present.
- Finally, when you have done all that you can do, ask God to help finish the process.

4

A Key to Your
College Education

The Internet

Happily Addicted to the Web
(Sung to the tune of "Winter Wonderland")

Doorbell rings, I'm not list'nin'
From my mouth, drool is glist'nin'
I'm happy—although
My boss let me go—
Happily addicted to the Web.

All night long, I sit clicking,
Unaware time is ticking,
There's beard on my cheek
Same clothes for a week,
Happily addicted to the Web.

Friends come by; they shake me,
Saying, "Yo, man!

Don't you know tonight's the senior prom?"
With a listless shrug, I mutter, "No, man;
I just discovered letterman-dot-com!"

I don't phone, don't send faxes,
Don't go out, don't pay taxes,
Who cares if someday
They drag me away?
I'm happily addicted to the Web!

source unknown

If you think this song makes no sense, you are one of the healthy ones who is not yet hooked on the Internet. If you chuckled as you read this song, it may already be too late. The most important new communication tool of the '90s, without a doubt, is the Internet. In fact, more than half of all students have Internet access and more than 75 percent of college campuses now access the Net. The average student will spend 123 percent more time on the Internet this year than last year, according to the December 1996 issue of *Prospectus*.

Students currently on the Net report sending four and receiving six e-mail messages on average a day, and that number is expected to increase dramatically in the future. Many residence halls are currently wired and offer Internet access in dorm rooms (actually anywhere there is a phone line, access through a computer modem is available). For example, at the University at Albany, three thousand residential students have access to the library; central computing services; and course materials, which include class notes, images, and lectures via the Web (see http://www.albany.edu).

Today, instead of being asked for your mailing address or phone number, you are just as likely to be asked for an e-mail address. The technology is changing so fast that I hesitate to write a chapter on this topic, because by the time this book comes out, the information will likely be outdated. Regardless, if you are not already aware of the powerful tool you have in the Internet to search for the college of your choice, this chapter is for you.

What Is the Internet?

Think of the Internet as a global network of approximately five million computers . . . and counting. In fact, by the time you read this, that number could easily have doubled. On the Internet is a global e-mail system and an information database called the World Wide Web (or simply the Web). While there are other resources on the Network, most of my comments will focus on e-mail and the Web.

Through a protocol called Transmission Control Protocol/Internet Protocol (TCP/IP), computers connected to the Internet can talk to each other and translate a vast variety of information. Connected via this Network are homes, colleges, businesses, churches, research institutes, government agencies, and just about any type of organization you can name. Many of these organizations provide information for others to read. Topics span anything you can think of and a whole lot of things you never imagined even existed. This information is accessible by way of an address, similar to a postal address, that usually starts with something like http://www.college.edu (not a real address).

The first computer screen you see when you access a Web address is called a home page, which usually has computer links to other areas and additional information. By clicking on underlined words in the text on the home page or by moving your cursor across the screen until the cursor becomes a little hand and then clicking, you can locate computer links to other information. This process of going from one screen to the next and viewing things of interest is commonly known as "surfing the Net."

The best way to learn the Internet is to have someone help you get set up and then look around for yourself at a variety of college home pages. Unlike early programming devices, the Internet is simple to navigate once someone gives you a brief introduction, because almost everything is simply a matter of pointing your cursor and clicking.

Organized in a free-form environment, there is no central index to the Internet and even if there were, it would be almost impossible to keep it updated, as the nature of the Network is ever changing. As a result, several tools have emerged on the Internet that will search for various topics when key words are given.

Hierarchical Guides and Indexes

A good place to start your Internet search for colleges is by accessing a general subject guide service. These services provide free access to all Internet users and are especially helpful when you are searching very broad topics or need to get a sense of the general resources that are available on the Network. Keep in mind that no one guide is a complete index to the Internet. Because of this you may need to look at several guides to get a comprehensive list of sources for your topic. The following are several popular guides with a brief description of some of the things you can expect to find related to your college education.

The Argus Clearinghouse

First time "surfers" may find the Argus Clearinghouse (http://www.clearinghouse.net) very informative and a good place to start. You will find a vast range of subject-specific guides that may help in your search. The Argus Clearinghouse rates each guide on a 1–5 scale so that you can determine the value of the guide before accessing it. The ratings are based on the following five criteria.

1. Resource description—factors such as how well the audience for the guide is described, how well the description of content is covered, and how often the guide is updated.
2. Resource evaluation—reliability of authors, quality of content, etc.
3. Guide design—quality of images, layout, and navigational aids.
4. Guide organizational schemes—how well they are organized by subject, audience, geography, authors, chronology, etc.
5. Meta-information—mission of the guide, how the guide was researched and constructed, information on the authors, etc.

Look in the general category of this guide under "education" at the home page for topics on issues such as adult education, distance education, disabilities, higher education, scholarships, and financial aid.

Yahoo

One of the older indexes to the Internet, Yahoo (http://www .yahoo.com), contains a vast range of index elements. More recent items added are marked in the margin by the word *new*. Students searching for colleges and related topics may do so by selecting the following topics in the index beginning with the home page. Select in the following order:

1. "Education-Universities" (brings you to index of universities around the world by country)
2. "Indices"
3. "College and University Home Pages" or "Colleges and Universities: All" (from here you can search for a particular school by selecting the first letter of its name)

You can also find massive data on issues related to college admission by selecting "Education-College Entrance" at the home page. Here you will find information on issues such as admissions offices, financial aid, online applications, and educational standards and testing.

The World Wide Web Virtual Library

The World Wide Web Virtual Library (http://www.w3.org/vl/) is an index that can be used to search educational topics in alphabetical order or by subject category. The quality of the narrative varies depending on the subject area. I found some descriptions very detailed while others appeared to be rather brief, but generally there is more information than is available in Yahoo. The site allows you to search under "education" alphabetically by site, educational level, resources provided, type of site, or country.

While searching by resources, for example, I came across Gutenberg College, a Christian college in Eugene, Oregon, which "provides a four-year liberal arts education in a Protestant Christian environment. The college uses a 'great books' curriculum emphasizing small-group discussions." While I cannot comment on reputation or quality of the school, the concept of reading classic books to develop basic learning skills (reading, writing, mathematics, and critical thinking) is one that I found intriguing (source: http://www.efn.org/~mscenter/guten/).

Search Engines and Finders

Most people who have used a computer in the library to find a particular author or used search words to do a research paper have already used a search engine. Basically a search engine is a software program that goes out and searches for a particular word or phrase across a large range of data.

For example, let's suppose you were interested in finding out everything about Stafford loans on the Internet. Since this is a rather specific search, I would start by calling up one of the search engines listed in this section and then type in the subject box the phrase "Stafford loan."

It is important to use quotation marks around the phrase "Stafford loan" because without them, most search engines will search and find anything that has to do with people named *Stafford* and companies with *Stafford* in their name, along with every type of real estate, car, and personal *loan* you can think of in the world. Without quotation marks, the computer could easily find ten thousand records that have to do with either the word *Stafford* or the word *loan*. By using quotation marks, you tell the computer you are searching for a phrase, not two independent words.

It is important to remember that while most search engines do the same basic function, there are some important differences. Some searches are done just on the titles of various sites while others search the full text of each document for your topic. You cannot assume that just because you ran a search engine on the

Internet, you have found all the relevant material available—for several reasons. First, due to their global nature and the millions of possible sites, search engines have not been designed to search every site available. Second, the Internet changes so rapidly that even if you updated your search index every day, there would still be sites added within minutes of your last update and others taken off the Internet. I would not be very surprised if several addresses in this book are no longer valid, though they were at the time of writing. For these reasons, if you want a comprehensive search, it makes sense to use more than one search engine.

Internet users get very accustomed to the words "No URL Found" when trying to access a site. This is computer lingo meaning simply that this site/address no longer exists. Another common response is "Web page not responding, try again later." This means one of two things: Either there are so many users trying to access the same site that there is no room, or the computer server is shut off at present.

Magellan

A good research source, Magellan (http://www.mckinley.com), is provided by international publishers and information specialists who write objective descriptions of family-oriented resources. You can search this database by key word and you can narrow your search by accessing only quality sites. Magellan rates sites with one to four stars, so you can search only three-star sites and above if you wish. Key words can also be designated to search a specific category, the entire database, or just those sites given the green light, which is Magellan's way of telling you the site is viewable by all ages. I am pleased to say that Magellan has tried to keep this source family oriented, so questionable material is not referenced from this engine. This, however, does not mean that all issues accessed through this search engine are appropriate for children.

Lycos

Arguably the largest search engine on the Internet, Lycos (http://www.lycos.com), searches FTP (file transfer protocol) and gopher sites in addition to WWW sites on the Internet. You don't need to know what all this means as long as you understand that this site searches a large portion of the Internet. Lycos will allow you to use functional searches with terms such as "= AND," "ALL," "= OR," and can match from two to seven terms. Detailed explanation on how to use these advanced search features is available online under "Boolean Expressions." It is also possible to designate how close a match you need and the level of detail. The best way to understand all this is to practice with a few searches before you need to do some serious research.

Alta Vista

The search engine called Alta Vista (http://altavista.digital.com) has the ability to do specific and unique searches. For example, a "+" sign can be used to designate terms you want included and a "-" sign can be used to select terms you do not wish to have included in the discussion. You would find this feature helpful if you wanted to search for topics related to Christian universities with women's basketball programs, exclusive of any men's programs.

Now that you have a general overview of some of the indexes and search engines available, the next step is to get online and experiment. Type in words or phrases about which you would like to have more information. Try names of schools or phrases, such as "college scholarships," "universities in (name of city or state)," "student financial aid," "collegiate athletic programs," "dorm life," and so on.

Sometimes your search will come up empty and sometimes you'll get more information than you bargained for. Just keep digging and you'll hit pay dirt sooner or later. At times you may reach a site that has material you cannot read until you download additional Internet software known as a "plug-in." Recently, while looking at Colorado Christian University's Web site, I found a cutting-edge online video. Since I did not have the proper plug-in software to watch the video, I quickly followed a link to the software manufacturer's site. There I was able to download the needed plug-in, free of charge, to my computer hard drive and then return to Colorado Christian's Web page. After several minutes of downloading the excellent admissions video itself, I was able to view it, without waiting for it to be mailed to me from the school.

Higher Education Sites You Should Know About

While most of the sites listed here unfortunately do not have videos to watch, they are worth your review.

Net Ministries

Net Ministries (http:/netministries.org/college.htm) provides a listing of Christian colleges and universities from a broad spectrum of denominations. When using this web index I found six Bethel colleges or theological seminaries. Each school has a link from Net Ministries to its home page.

National Christian College Athletic Association

If you are an athlete or a student interested in various sports programs, the National Christian College Athletic Association's site (http://www.bright.net/~nccaa/) will provide you with a list of Christian colleges and universities that have been tournament winners in cross country, volleyball, soccer, basketball, wrestling, golf, tennis, baseball, and track. This could be a good start in a search to identify Christian schools with a strong program in your sport. Keep in mind that not all Christian colleges participate in this association, but it is a good place to begin.

Forecasting College Costs

The Forecasting College Costs site (http://www.salliemae.com/calculators/costs/) is a great resource to help you calculate how much you will need to attend school. This is also good for future projections if you are reading this several years before you plan to attend college. This calculator can also project what your expected family contribution will need to be after financial aid. This is worth checking out, although first-time reviewers may find the costs of college a little depressing.

Coalition for Christian Colleges and Universities

The Coalition's site (http://www.cccu.org) is a good place to begin any college search. The home page provides links to more than ninety Christian colleges and universities across the United States and Canada. If you are interested in the specific materials used for instruction in an area in which you might wish to major, there is a section titled "Resources for Teaching at Coalition Colleges and Universities," which gives you links to various work being done in a wide variety of disciplines at Christian colleges. Also of interest is a section titled "Choosing the College That Is Right for You," which contains a map of schools in each part of the country and a list of schools by denomination.

Test Prep

Test Prep (http://www.testprep.com/) is a free resource for SAT test-taking preparation. A complete test preparation program with more than seven hundred practice problems that come from actual tests is provided. The first time through you are asked to take an actual SAT test so that your weak areas can be identified. From there questions are designed to strengthen these areas. Tell Mom and Dad you will be spending some time on the computer and tying up a phone line if you decide to go this route for your SAT review. The plan is for this site to have review programs for GMAT, GRE, LSAT, and TOEFL in the future as well.

Nellie Mae

No, Nellie Mae is not your mother's rich cousin who wants to give you some money. Nellie Mae (http://www.nelliemae.org/)

is the largest nonprofit provider of student loans in the United States. The Nellie Mae home page has helpful information on understanding the college loan process, various options available to students, early college planning materials, loan comparison charts, and repayment information. This is a good financial aid information resource, even if you're not related to Nellie Mae.

CIBC Student Center

CIBC Student Center (http://www.cibc.com/needs/student/) is a resource for Canadian students in need of information related to financial aid programs, student loans, and CIBC personal student loans. Canadian students can also search for schools by province with direct links to college and university Web pages.

U.S. Department of Education

A large number of materials, reports, and studies done by the U.S. Department of Education is available online at http://www.ed.gov. Of particular interest to you may be the section titled "The Student Guide to Financial Aid," which contains information on Pell grants, Direct and FFEL Stafford loans, PLUS loans, consolidated loans, along with eligibility requirements, deadlines, and telephone numbers. This is a good source for current government data.

Internet College Exchange

The Internet College Exchange (http://www.usmall.com/college/) is a site with free membership, which provides a search service for high school students and their families. The Internet College Exchange allows students to search all the colleges in the United States to help make an educated decision about where they would like to go to school. There is information on such things as distance learning, scholarships, and access to newsletters. When I clicked on several of the options while writing this book, some were still under construction, but this site has promise.

The Down Side of the Internet

As with any new technology there are opportunities on the Internet for abuses in the college admissions process. For example, providers have surfaced who, for a fee, will provide a variety of more than one thousand essays written by successful applicants to prestigious institutions. One such company pays twenty-five to seventy-five dollars for an essay written by a student who has been admitted to college and is willing to sell the essay. Buyers pay ten to sixty dollars for a packet of five to ten essays that claims to "give students some insight into what admissions committees consider a good essay and provides them with ideas to inspire their own writing."[1]

While at first glance this may sound like a great idea, it presents a great temptation to use someone else's words in your own essay. This would be plagiarism. Be very careful if you decide to access one of these services lest your decision result in the downfall of an otherwise bright future. Many colleges will not only reject applications when they find borrowed words, but they may also contact the applicant's high school. Even if you feel the risk of anyone ever finding out is minimal, God will know that it wasn't your work. Enough said.

5

Interviewing
a College Recruiter

Twelve Questions to Ask

It's not unlikely that when you make your first visit to a college campus, you will be greeted by a recruiter. Often this will be the same person you have already spoken to by phone, or perhaps met at a college booth. These clean-cut, all-American university representatives are usually recent graduates who were student campus leaders. Guiding you around campus for the first time, one of their goals will be to answer any questions you have about the university. To help you ask the best questions, I have prepared some that will leave even the best recruiters stumped and amazed at your insightful inquiries. (Unless, of course, they have read this book. Then they will find you thorough but predictable.)

My guess is that the average recruiter will not have ready answers to all of the questions I am suggesting. This is because he or she will be expecting the questions posed by most potential students, questions that deal primarily with weekend activities and which night they serve pizza in the cafeteria. Don't get me wrong—recreation and food are important issues, particularly if your main goal during your college years is to enjoy sunsets and gain weight. However, if a great college education is what you're after, try asking a few of these other questions as well.

1. *Is this a teaching or research university?*

Imagine for a moment that it is your first day of college. You spend an extra ten minutes in front of the mirror to make sure that when you meet the perfect date you are looking your best. After breakfast, you make your way over to your first class and check the number on the door three times to make sure it is the right room. You are fifteen minutes early (this will probably never happen again) and as you walk into the room, you notice that you are actually in what appears to be a small auditorium. So that you can see everyone in the room, you position yourself in a prime spot in the back row. Soon other students start coming in until there are more than two hundred people in the room. Everyone is talking, and you hardly notice a young woman in her twenties writing her name on the board and handing out papers. The papers turn out to be your syllabus and the young woman turns out to be a graduate student who has been assigned to teach your class. Welcome to what we call a *research university.*

While you can receive a good education at either a research university or its counterpart, the *teaching university,* there are some philosophical differences between the two systems that will impact your classroom experience. Theoretically at a research university faculty are hired for two reasons: to teach students and to conduct and publish research designed to contribute to their field of knowledge and also to promote the reputation of the university. Behind the scenes, however, most faculty know that being published is of primary priority if they hope to advance in rank and even to keep their job. As a result, much of their time when they are not in the classroom is spent writing journal articles for scholarly publications. Due to this pressure to publish, it may be hard to find these experienced professors during office hours or outside of class.

In fact, even classroom hours provide no guarantee of contact with these experienced faculty. Often research universities attract some of the best and brightest young graduate students, because at the graduate level much of the faculty research really does pay off for the students. A common way for these graduate students to pay for their education is to teach classes for faculty members. Unfortunately for the freshman class, these inexperienced graduate students often end up teaching the introductory courses in large lecture halls. If you are a student who hopes to have considerable contact with a mentor teacher, this may not be your type of school. Although there are exceptions to what I am describing, as a rule with this kind of system it is not likely that most undergraduate students will have much contact with the faculty.

In contrast, a school that is considered a teaching university will often have less of an academic publishing reputation but more of a focus on teaching. Classes tend to be smaller, and the faculty tend to be hired for their teaching ability rather than their ability to conduct and publish research. Of course, research is still encouraged, but it very often doesn't materialize due to the fact that faculty in teaching universities tend to spend most of their time in the classroom, teaching nine to fifteen hours a week (in contrast, faculty at research schools typically teach six to nine hours each week). Also, faculty at teaching universities are more generalist in nature and tend to teach a wider range of classes. While they may have a better idea of how all the various academic areas fit together, they may not be quite as knowledgeable in a specific field as you would find at a research university.

There is a place for both types of university, but from my experience I have come to favor the teaching university for the undergraduate student, either type school for the master's degree student, and the research university for the doctoral student.

2. *What is the student/faculty ratio?*
The student/faculty ratio is a measure of class size. A 25 to 1 student/faculty ratio would mean that the average class at the university would have twenty-five students to one instructor. Generally the lower the ratio the better, but I guess that all depends on whether or not you want a professor looking over your shoul-

der. The ratio given by a college can be deceptive in that some universities have very large introductory classes balanced by rather small classes for seniors and graduate students. The overall result may be a much lower student/faculty ratio than you actually experience in your first- or second-year classes. For this reason, it would be wise to ask for the student/faculty ratio in the freshman year or for a particular group of classes that you plan to take.

If the recruiter isn't able to provide this data, a call to the registrar's office will be very informative. Pick out a few of the first-year courses that you would be taking if enrolled and find out the current class sizes. (Oh, and don't forget to be very kind to the person you talk to in the registrar's office as you make this request, because it may appear to him or her to be a meaningless exercise.)

3. *May I see a copy of your annual crime report?*

Most cities keep a record of crimes committed during the year, and universities have similar reports for their campuses. You, by law, have access to these reports. Since the last thing a recruiter wants to do is scare you, it is not likely that this information will be offered unless you make a specific request. Security is extremely important in this day and age and should not be overlooked as one factor in your college choice.

For example, UCLA reported 1,654 offenses in 1995. The vast majority of these were thefts. Keep in mind that larger schools will have more crimes due to their size but may not actually be any more dangerous than a smaller institution. Check the ratio of the number of students enrolled to crimes committed to get a more accurate picture when comparing crime reports. It also helps to know how many of the violent crimes actually occurred on campus as opposed to crimes that occurred in the surrounding neighborhood. This may affect where you decide to live.

If you are living at home, the incidence of crime may not be much of a concern, but if you are staying on campus, this information is a must. Some related issues to consider are the neighborhood surrounding the school, number of access roads in and out of the school, how well the campus is patrolled at night, security gates, and dorm access after hours.

If the school does not provide crime statistics, the local police should be able to provide some unbiased information to help you evaluate the safety of the area.

4. *May I have a copy of last year's or this year's chapel schedule?*

Whether or not a school convenes its students for chapel will tell you something about how serious they are about providing a spiritual experience on campus. Furthermore, by reviewing a school's chapel schedule for this year or last year, you can probably learn something about the kind of chapel experience that is offered. As you evaluate the speakers, music, and special events that have been provided in the past, consider the following:

- Some universities make an effort to expose students to a wide range of spiritual experiences, while others are more concerned with indoctrination.
- Some universities favor an intellectual or informational experience, while others provide a worship experience.
- In some chapels student involvement is evident, and in others administration and faculty seem to control things.

You may be able to tell from the chapel schedule the school's stand on these issues. If the recruiter is a former student of the university, he or she may also be able to give some insights about what to expect from chapel. This will be helpful in finding a school that provides the spiritual growth you are looking for. Again, don't expect the recruiter to have a copy of the chapel schedule on his or her desk. You may have to contact the university chaplain or office of student affairs for this information.

5. *What religious groups meet on campus?*

Every campus I have visited—whether or not it is a Christian university—has religious groups meeting on or around the campus. If your recruiter doesn't know the answer to this question, the best way to get this information is to check out the bulletin boards around campus. Most campus Bible studies and fellowships post meeting times in the cafeteria and on other public boards. If you come up empty after a careful search, check with the university chaplain or try running an ad in the campus newspaper requesting information about specific types of groups meeting on campus. There are often various ethnic and special-interest fellowship groups from which to choose. For example, on our campus we have a group that call themselves the Christian Cowboy Fellowship. You have to wear a cowboy hat and boots and brand your calves with the initials JC to join (okay, so I was kidding about the calves). You may also be able to get some help regarding meeting times and places from an Internet search.

6. Do you have a campus newspaper and can I subscribe in advance?

This is a great source of information from the student's perspective about what is happening at the university. Generally a subscription for the year is relatively cheap and often fun to read. After a year of reading the campus news, you may feel like you know the campus. After all, where else can you find out about the frog belching contest or that the hamburger buns in the snack bar taste like sweat socks? These are things a student has to know! Seriously, there are some good insights into campus life to be gleaned from the school newspaper that you won't find anywhere else.

7. Can you show me the type of room I would have if I live on campus?

Don't let them show you only the newest dorm on campus, unless you would be staying there. Also, it's always better to see a room that is in use rather than an empty room, so you can get an idea of how the space would actually work with roommate(s). In addition, walking down a hall and glancing into open doorways can be . . . well, let's just say it can be revealing. Imagine thirty teenagers on the same floor of a dorm with no mom around to tell them to pick things up or wash their clothes or make their bed. It's not always a pretty sight, but it is "freedom"!

Also make sure you ask how many roommates you would have in each room you see. If campus housing gets overloaded, it's not uncommon for freshmen to end up with more people in the room than was originally intended when the dorm was built.

8. *What are the best examples of God's presence on this campus?*

Try asking this question of several people on campus to see what the spiritual dimensions are of the university. If the school has a strong spiritual focus, this will not be a difficult question for people to answer. Unfortunately many schools say they provide a Christian atmosphere, but it is very difficult for them to explain what they mean by that beyond the fact that women are not allowed to spend the night in the men's dorms and there is no drinking or smoking on campus.

At Dallas Baptist University, for example, there is a strong focus on servant leadership. Some of the evidence of this includes the following: a prominent bronze statue in the center of campus depicting Christ as a servant leader, specific "servant leadership" wording in our mission statement, orientation speakers who explain the importance of this concept to incoming students, Christian service days when students are encouraged to meet the needs of someone less fortunate than they are, freshmen orientation classes where servant leadership is discussed in depth, biblical references made in chapel, and so on. And these are only a few small examples of the spiritual emphasis that can be found on the DBU campus!

Each school, particularly if it claims to be a Christian institution, has its own way of expressing God's relationship to people and, if it is clearly done, you should see the footprints all over campus. The best way, however, to see God's presence on any campus is in the hearts of the students. Sit in the cafeteria for a few minutes and talk to students about God and you will quickly see if he is brightly shining at the university. I can assure you there are schools where God's light *does* shine.

9. *What are the strongest majors at this college?*

If you are planning to major in, oh, let's say, education, you are not just looking for a recruiter to assure you that they offer that major on campus. What you want is a strong program. Most people don't go to Kentucky Fried Chicken for fish—even though it may be on the menu—because KFC is known for chicken. This is also true of colleges. Most schools have a wide range of programs but cannot support all of them to the same degree. As a result, pockets of excellence tend to develop.

How do you find these pockets of excellence? You might say to yourself that since ABC University has a large number of students in a communications program, it must be a strong program. While in most cases this is an indicator of a strong program, it may also be an indicator that this is the easiest program on campus. There are some excellent small programs on most campuses where serious students can get a lot of attention from faculty in a very personalized environment.

One good indicator is to contact people in the community around the university. Locate leaders who work in the field in which you are interested in majoring and ask where they go to find new employees. For example, if you want to study nursing, contact the personnel department at a local hospital and ask if they look favorably on hiring graduates from the school you are considering.

It may also help to see how graduates fare in getting into graduate schools, medical programs, and law schools. The recruiter and faculty should be able to locate some statistics on this. If, however, you are not sure you are getting the whole story, try doing your own research. Go to the campus library, obtain a university yearbook from about five years ago, and look up the names of several students at random who graduated in your area of interest. You want alumni who have been out of college long enough to have discovered how well they were prepared for their careers—yet not so long ago that the program and faculty would have changed dramatically. Then ask the alumni office to help you locate these people with phone numbers—they should be happy to help. Hopefully, by the time you have finished your research, you will have gained confidence in the program you have selected.

10. *What percentage of the faculty have doctorates and how many are alumni of the university?*

Most colleges and universities have statistics on the number of their faculty who have a doctorate in their field. This is a good indicator of how qualified the faculty are to teach at the college level. As a loose rule of thumb, I would not consider any college where fewer than half of the full-time faculty have doctoral degrees in their field. In addition to having a significant number of doctorates, in some fields such as business, nursing, computer science, and education, you want to have a significant number of faculty who currently work or have recently worked in the field. Part-time faculty, also known as adjunct faculty, add a very healthy dimension to the learning environment when they are currently working in the areas in which they teach. Part-time faculty working in the field are not as likely to have a doctorate, so a healthy balance of both full- and part-time faculty is optimal for a good education.

And while we're talking about faculty, let's test your knowledge. Is it good for most of the faculty to be graduates from the university where they teach? Believe it or not, while this may appear to show alumni loyalty, it is not a good sign to have more than about 20 percent of the faculty with their last degree coming from the same school where they teach. This can be a sign of a school that has either isolated itself from the rest of the academic community or has not been successful in attracting quality graduates from other reputable universities. At the far extreme, this is a common characteristic of degree mills—institutions that practically give away degrees (very often by mail order!). In any case, a high number of faculty with their doctorate from the same school where they teach should serve as a warning signal in your search.

11. *Does the school have graduate programs and if so, in what area?*
Who cares, right? The last thing you're probably interested in right now is graduate school, but believe it or not, it is a factor that needs to be considered in school selection. Graduate programs at a school that you are considering can be both a good and a bad sign. A school having a graduate program in your major can indicate a strong faculty that students may benefit from at both the graduate and undergraduate level. Plus, if you decide to go on to graduate school, you can often do so with relatively little interruption since you are already familiar with the campus and have hopefully established numerous friendships.

On the other hand, there are some schools where the best faculty are siphoned from the undergraduate program to meet the needs of the graduate school. Students beginning their education on these campuses may find themselves at the mercy of graduate students and a lesser qualified faculty.

To help sort all this out, an interview with the academic dean responsible for the area in which you want to study may provide some insight. Some deans believe that only the best faculty should be assigned to entry-level courses because these are the classes where students make decisions about majoring in a particular field of study. These deans may argue that many students make career decisions in the introductory classes based on a teacher who opened up a whole new world to them.

If, however, the dean has the attitude that more experienced students need better teachers to challenge them, then there may be a tendency to put new and weaker faculty in the introductory courses so that the best faculty can teach the senior and graduate-level courses. Some schools have an unwritten policy of giving graduate faculty smaller course loads and more research assistants, which can have the effect of encouraging the better faculty of the institution to teach graduate-level courses.

Hopefully, understanding both the strengths and weaknesses associated with graduate schools on a college campus will allow you to make a better decision.

12. *May I have a copy of your student handbook?*

You may be about as interested in reading student handbooks as you are in reading *Webster's Dictionary.* However, some of the best indicators of how you will fit in at a given college or university are available in the student handbook. Many students, expelled from universities for campus violations, would have survived on another campus that fit them better. They should have done some research before enrolling.

In the student handbook you will find such gems as dorm rules, dress codes, how to appeal a grade, social clubs, and even whether or not a refrigerator is allowed in your dorm room. On a deeper level, the handbook often gives you a sense of the university climate on matters related to coed dorm visitation, gay rights, university mission, attitudes toward alcohol and drugs, and the overall spiritual climate. As you read, try not to get lost in any legal wording, but concentrate instead on getting an overall picture of the university.

Ironically, as important as the handbook is to understanding the university, it is often not given out by the admissions staff unless specifically requested. Careful review of this document will quickly distinguish one institution from another and is a must for any serious university analysis.

Below is a list of topics you can expect to find in a typical student handbook:

Alcohol and drug policy
Cafeteria hours
Chapel hours and attendance (if applicable)
Computer lab hours
Disability issues
Dress codes
Library hours and privileges
Library services
Misconduct appeals
Professional counseling
Student associations and clubs
Student curfew (if applicable)
Student government
Student insurance and health care
University sports

Of course, it's not mandatory that you ask each of these twelve questions to make a wise choice of college and have a good experience there. Yet there's no denying that the more of this kind of information you can obtain, the greater your chances of matching your interests with just the right college or university.

The important thing to remember when asking questions at this stage is not to feel afraid or embarrassed to raise these issues or others about which you may be concerned. After all, you will be investing a significant sum of time, money, and energy at whatever institution you choose to attend. So speak up. Well-planned questions today can mean a better college experience in the years to come.

6

Fee, Fie, Foe, Fum, I Smell the Room of a College Freshman

The Campus Visit

You've just entered a zone where people cheer when they don't receive what they pay for (class is canceled), where people are on a different time than those in the rest of the world (average waking hours: 10 A.M. to 2 P.M.), where people's attire doesn't necessarily reflect the event (everything else is dirty), and where everyone agrees on one thing (cafeteria food stinks). No, this is not the "twilight zone" . . . this is college. Should you choose to venture into this zone, be prepared for the strange, the wonderful, and the downright gross.

During my college days, one of the guys on my floor put medicine on his feet each night that, when combined with toe jam, would have gagged even a roach. The chemists on the floor unsuccessfully tried to replicate the reaction in the lab to see if an antiserum could be found. When the yell went down the floor, "Here it comes!" all doors slammed shut, and if time permitted, all air holes around the door were taped in an effort at survival. Ever studied with a gas mask on? Okay, it wasn't quite that bad, but this was a real problem on our freshman floor.

Hopefully you won't experience anything like this on a campus visit, but still a campus overnight can be very revealing. Once you have narrowed your list of potential schools down to three or four, it is time to visit. Most schools are set up to offer a weekend of activities aimed at attracting future students. Students are invited to visit classes, eat in the cafeteria, meet college students, sleep in a residence hall, attend lectures, and enjoy social events. These overnights will often confirm your desire to attend a particular school or get you excited about college if you are not already motivated to begin the college experience.

Campus Signals

While you are enjoying yourself, don't forget to look for some of the following little signs on campus:

Graffiti. Generally the graffiti or the absence of graffiti is a good indicator of what kind of campus you are visiting. If you don't believe me, try this strange experiment. Visit a state university residence hall and read the comments written in several of the bathroom stalls and then go to a Christian university and do the same thing. (Warning: It could be dangerous to open the bathroom door and ask residents to leave so you can read their graffiti.) I have found that while there are some of the same types of comments on both campuses, in most cases there is much less graffiti at a Christian school and when it does exist, it sometimes is Christian in nature. I have even seen theological debates going back and forth alongside the toilet paper rolls on some campuses! Think about it for a moment. The graffiti says a lot about the students on that floor, so if the writing on the walls in a "Christian" college is no different than in a public rest room, then it's probably a campus where the lifestyles of the students are not much different than those of the secular world.

Chapel or prayer room. Does one exist and if so, does it show any signs of being used? Chapels and prayer rooms that are locked most of the day indicate that they see little activity. Are there any current prayer requests posted? Are there any sign-up times and if so, how many names are there? The absence of such a devotional area or one showing little use may be worth noting in your visit.

Bulletin boards. The notices tacked on bulletin boards can give you a sense of what happens on campus. Do you find only parties mentioned or are there Christian service groups advertising things like inner-city ministry, church events, Bible studies, and Christian fellowship? Don't get me wrong, I think there should be game nights and a variety of social events, but the absence of Christian small-group activities posted on campus bulletin boards would be a serious warning signal for me.

Concerts. What musical group is coming to campus? This can provide yet another clue to the quality of campus life.

Cars on campus. The first thing I notice on most of the college campuses I visit is that the student parking lot has nicer cars in it than the faculty lot. But look a little closer at these student cars. Do you see fish symbols or a skull and crossbones in the window? What is on the bumper stickers? What can you see in the backseats—Bibles and old church bulletins or beer cans and *Playboy* magazines?

Mealtimes. Look around the cafeteria and see how many students pray before they eat. Recently I was on a "Christian" campus and noticed that the whole time I sat in the faculty dining area, no one prayed.

Profanity. Are you hearing a lot of profanity on campus? Do the faculty use curse words in their lectures? Is it common language in the dorm? Ask around and see how common this is on campus. Again, I hate to say this, but at a secular conference, I was approached by a faculty member from another "Christian" college. Despite the fact that he knew I was from a Christian school, he cursed more than anyone I met that week.

It is important to note that many strong Christian colleges do not require all of their students to be Christians and even on campuses where everyone signs a statement of faith, there are non-believers. As a result, no Christian campus will come out clean in all these areas. In fact, most of the world's problems exist even on the best of campuses, because we are human. The key here is whether or not these negative elements dominate the campus to the point where the tone of the community is affected. You should be able to tell, over the course of a weekend, whether or not God is really alive on the campus you visit. If you are visiting a non-Christian college, you should have a sense as to what Christian campus groups are active on campus and whether or not the atmosphere would be hostile toward your faith.

The Faculty: Hello, Is Anybody Home?

The academic credentials of faculty are important, but just as important is the accessibility of the faculty. Try walking through the faculty office area to see if anyone is home during your campus visit. It is important to do this on a weekday during normal working hours to see who is in their office. Keep in mind that faculty do not, nor should they be expected to, spend all their working hours in their office, but there should be some signs of life. Some faculty areas appear about as desolate and uninhabited as the moon; you can see old remnants indicating that someone was there and left something behind many years ago, but no one has been around recently. Look on the doors for posted office hours. It would be normal to expect eight to ten office hours posted per week. Less than this could be a warning signal as to how available the faculty really are. If you happen to be visiting during scheduled faculty office hours, is the faculty member in?

You can also look for signs of Christian study materials or Bibles. If an office is open, you may be able to see such materials on the shelves or on the desk. If a teacher is taking the concept of integrating faith with learning seriously, there should be some supporting evidence.

Since mentoring is also a very important part of the college experience, it is always helpful to look for faculty in the discipline you plan to pursue who are of the same gender that you are. Historically some disciplines have been dominated by men or women, so this may not always be an indicator of sensitivity to gender but rather a reflection of the type of faculty available in a given field. For example, there are generally very few male faculty in most schools of nursing and very few female faculty in most schools of engineering.

Along these same lines, if you are a member of a minority group, it may be helpful to look for faculty who represent your group. At the same time, please keep in mind that, due to the fact that some ethnic or minority groups offer a proportionately small number of doctorally qualified faculty, the lack of representatives on campus may have more to do with lack of availability than discrimination. If you are a minority, you may wish to set a goal to one day return as a faculty member to your college to mentor others.

The Library: Silence Is Golden

Since most learning revolves around the library, it would be a mistake not to check out this area while on campus. Don't worry. I'm not going to ask you to evaluate the number of works by Plato or Thoreau. The criteria I have in mind are of a more practical nature.

Begin by paying attention to the atmosphere in the library. Is it a place where people party or is it a place where you could study without distraction?

Second, how computerized is the library system? The number of bookshelves and floors in a library can be misleading because libraries today are moving to online databases with full-text availability where you will be able to do word searches within entire books or magazines instead of reading each page. Most libraries have their card files on computer today, but you can expect more. The most efficient research library I have seen to date was in one room about the size of a classroom. Most of the area was taken up by computer terminals and printers while the library resources were maintained by off-site computer data banks that were shared with many other organizations, keeping costs at a minimum.

If you want to test the library resources at your prospective university, try going into the library with a couple of research topics in mind and asking the research librarian to show you how to research each topic in the library. Does the librarian refer you to the archives of books in the attic or does he or she sit you down with a computer to search a CD-ROM? Actually, both types of resource are helpful. See how long it takes to find materials that you could use for a class project and how helpful the library staff are.

Please note that I mentioned library research here because I believe that, despite the growing influence of technology like the Internet, there will always be a need for books. For one thing, people will continue to want to read while resting beside a lake or while relaxing on a trip. But also, many of us comprehend more when reading the printed page than when reading a computer screen. I'll probably live to eat my words, but it's hard to imagine a class where the only resource is a computer and highlighting key passages requires the use of a mouse!

The Residence Hall: You Need to Experience It to Believe It

If you will be traveling a long distance to visit a particular university, make the effort to visit campus during a "normal" weekend in addition to any other specialty weekends you visit—such as high school preview or homecoming weekends—even if it means making two trips! All campuses plan a smorgasbord of exciting events during special weekends. But normal weekends are much more telling. During an average weekend, some campuses offer lots of activities for residents, while other campuses turn into ghost towns as the majority of their residents commute to nearby hometowns.

It is important to see the residence hall at 2 A.M. as well as at 2 P.M., when the admissions counselor is more likely to give you a tour. On some campuses certain floors are designated as quiet floors for students who want to go to bed and actually get some sleep. For other students, a big part of college is the games and social events that happen late at night.

Finally, even though the price of a room may not vary much between residence halls, the amount of space and quality of living conditions can vary dramatically on the same campus. Often freshmen get last choice of rooms, but it still doesn't hurt to know what the room options are and make a request for your first choice. For example, a room at the end of the hall usually has more windows and less noise, since you don't have neighbors on both sides. How far you are from the lobby, bathroom, or lounge can also make a major difference in the noise level in your room. Older residence halls may have less-modern facilities, but sometimes they have larger rooms, which can be helpful if you have a U-Haul full of clothes and other belongings.

On large campuses some dorms will be considerably closer to where most of your classes are than others. On a below-zero morning or a day when you wake up late for class, the distance to class may become a serious issue.

If a residence hall has several floors, you will want to request the floor as well. My suggestion in most residence halls is the second floor. It is far enough off the ground so that you don't have people looking in or banging on or climbing in your window (they do all the above), but you also won't get winded every time you climb the stairs to your room. You will understand exactly what I'm talking about if you ever get assigned to the fifth floor of a residence hall without an elevator when it comes time to move in and out of your room. Even with an elevator, which can get busy, you may have to take the stairs just to save some time.

The Cafeteria: The Universal Letdown

Although there are some great meals on university campuses, food is generally not rated by most students as a highlight of the college experience. In other words, the food stinks! Let's face it; it is very difficult to cook for several thousand students and make each one feel like Mom has just made a home-cooked meal.

A campus visit to the cafeteria can often be misleading for the following reasons:

1. Often special food is prepared for university events such as a high school weekend, so you don't get the traditional menu.
2. Sometimes it is not the quality of food, but the lack of variety that is so difficult for students. Some college cafeterias prepare the same meal over and over several times a week, but for the first-time visitor, the food seems fine.

Regardless of your experience visiting the cafeteria, if you don't go off to college with high expectations, you may avoid some disappointment when it comes to meals.

Recreational and Sports Facilities: How Much Is Really Available?

If you are into sports and exercise, the availability of recreational facilities may influence your decision to attend a particular school. Don't be impressed, however, by all the great facilities on any campus until you find out who can use them. On many campuses the athletic teams monopolize the best facilities, which means that much of the equipment you see on a campus tour is seldom available to the rest of the student population. Also, the geographic region of the country where you plan to go to school affects the type of facility you need. For example, if you attend a college in Minnesota, you may need an indoor track more than at a college in Florida.

Buildings That Are Skipped on the Campus Tour

It is traditional during most campus visits to have a tour of the university. You will probably visit such places as the acoustically perfect symphony hall with the cherry wood floor imported from Spain and the pipe organ from Poland, which was donated by the Lottawealth family in memory of their dog Mitsy.

By the way, have you ever noticed how tour guides seem to need to tell you what country things came from? It's as if everyone knows that Spain is a very good source of cherry wood. When I am on a tour like this, I fight the urge to take off my shirt and display the tag while exclaiming, "This shirt is 100 percent cotton, made in China!"

My point is, who cares?

But back to the symphony hall. This may be an impressive facility if you are a music major, but the truth is that if you are majoring in some other discipline, you may not find yourself in such a hall more than once or twice during your college career. The places you need to visit are those you will see every day. The problem is that often these places are not on the designated tour. Every school wants to showcase its prize facilities and minimize its weak spots.

I've heard recruiters say that they try to keep students out of the cafeteria, for example, or the bookstore or student center, because it is not one of the bright spots on their campus. I've provided a checklist below for your campus tour. It will help you make sure that all areas of specific interest are covered in a campus visit regardless of what is on the traditional tour. It makes much more sense for you to decide what you want to see than to depend on a recruiter to anticipate your interests.

Campus Tour Checklist

All Students

__Auditorium for chapel
__Bookstore
__Cafeteria/snack bar
__Campus health center
__Classrooms
__Computer labs
__Freshmen parking area
__Freshmen residence halls

__Gymnasium
__Library
__Mailboxes
__Prayer room
__Registration areas
__Student center
__Writing lab

Athletics and Kinesiology
__Golf, bowling,
  and other facilities
__Jogging track(s)
__Locker rooms (general purpose)
__Sport medicine facility
__Swimming pool
__Tennis and racquetball courts
__Vans/buses for travel to sports
  events
__Weight room

*Broadcast, Speech,
and Print Communications*
__Campus newspaper offices
__Campus radio station
__Darkroom
__Speech pathology lab
__Tape editing bay
__TV control room and studio

Facilities for Physically Challenged
__Bathroom facilities
__Classrooms
__Computer-assisted
  learning center
__Elevators
__Office for the physically
  challenged
__Parking
__Ramps
__Readers
__Residence halls

Languages
__Language faculty offices
__Language labs
__Travel abroad programs office

Music and Drama
__Auditorium control booth
__Choir rehearsal rooms
__Computer music facilities
__Costume room/storage
__Fine arts center
__Lighting
__Musical instruments
__Music building classrooms
__Music faculty offices
__Music lockers
__Orchestra pit
__Practice rooms
__Recording equipment
__Senior recital room
__Sheet music library

Science and Computers

__Anatomy and biology models   __Observatory

__Computer science faculty offices   __Science faculty offices

__Hardware and software   __Science labs
   inventory

A well-planned campus visit will be invaluable in helping you select a college. I strongly recommend making one campus visit during a preview weekend, followed by a trip to campus during a couple of "normal" days. Be vocal about what you want to see, find out what options you have in the way of residence life, and look for subtle signs of campus health. Regardless of what you find, you have a great excuse to get out of high school classes for a couple of days!

7

A Match Made in Heaven

How to Know a Christian College When You See One

A Christian college? All I can say is "Wow!" It's such a blessing to attend a Christian college. Every day I'm reminded how awesome God really is. Professors relate subject matter to God's principles and teachings. In many classes there's a time for prayer. When I am on campus, I feel God's presence constantly. It's really an uplifting experience.

Sarah Moffett, college freshman

One of the most perplexing questions asked by students and parents is how to identify a Christian college or university. Having spent considerable time at some very good Christian colleges and universities, I can tell you I haven't seen a halo over any faculty heads or an angel hovering around the baseball field, but there are signs that will help in the selection process. My experience is that students and parents truly don't know what to expect when they begin the search for a Christian college.

What Is a Christian College?

Here are some of the misunderstandings I often encounter regarding Christian schools.

Kum Ba Ya College

After preview weekends when high school students stay in residence halls and experience days full of fun activities mixed with devotional experiences, students often expect college to be an extended summer church camp experience. The Christian college campus is also often the site for a band, cheerleading, or other summer camp, so students arrive at college prepared for a nightly campfire complete with the singing of "Kum Ba Ya." Then when the first wave of exams hits, the students feel like they're holding their head underwater and are not able to come up for air. Trust me, college will likely be some of the best years of your life, but a dose of freshman English, calculus, and U.S. history taught from a Christian perspective is no church camp.

Once a Christian College, Always a Christian College (Not!)

I don't know how many times I have heard or read the phrase "founded on a Christian heritage," describing a private university. This is not really a distinguishing characteristic of a Christian college, because almost every private college or university in America was founded by a Christian denomination. In fact, of the first 119 universities established in the United States, 104 of them were founded by Christians. For example, Dartmouth was a mission to the Indians, and Princeton originated from a Christian initiative called the Great Awakening.

Christian Leadership Ministries reports that the earliest account of the founding of Harvard College included the following statement:

> Let every student be plainly instructed and earnestly pressed to consider well the main end of his life and studies is to know God and Jesus Christ which is life eternal . . .

In fact, for the first one hundred years, all of Harvard's faculty were also ministers.

Sadly, now on many campuses the chapel is more of a historical landmark than a statement of the university's spiritual commitment. There is more to a Christian school than pretty stained glass windows.

The Biblical Monastery or Convent

Some people seem to get the idea that when they walk onto a Christian college campus, they are going to see monks scurrying about, chanting or crouched in some antique room copying the latest version of the Bible with quill and scroll. People are often surprised when I tell them that the largest academic program on the Dallas Baptist University campus is business and that we are teaching two-way interactive video classes in off-campus corporations. On most Christian campuses today, Bible, while it is the center of integration in every field of study, would not make the top ten in terms of the number of students selecting it as a major. The fact is that Christian institutions offer the same wide range of specializations found on secular campuses. Unfortunately many Christian students eliminate Christian schools from their list of options because they wrongly assume that these campuses offer little more than Bible classes.

I Thought This Was Supposed to Be a Christian University

When the admissions counselor doesn't send the information requested or the receptionist is not as friendly as he or she should be, the assumption is that the college is not the Christian organization it was thought to be. Many people visualize Christian colleges as heavenly environments peopled by friendly, caring men and women who perfectly exemplify the servant image. Then when they encounter someone who occasionally shows his or her human side, they feel let down.

It is important to understand in your search for the right Christian school that all campuses—Christian or not—have their share of Scrooges. Be careful not to dismiss a good opportunity because of one grouchy or rude person on any campus.

Some Good Indicators of a Christian College or University

Enough about some of the common misunderstandings about Christian colleges and universities. Let's take a look at seven specific things you can look for that will help you determine if a college or university truly offers a Christ-focused environment.

1. Faculty and Staff Who Profess Faith in Jesus Christ

First and foremost, all the faculty and staff at a Christian college should share the common bond of having a personal relationship with Jesus Christ. Even in secular organizations, administrators insist on having their workers all buy into the mission and vision of the organization. I have never understood how Christian schools could achieve their mission without employing Christians who practice and believe in that mission. In my mind it is a sad development when a Christian school—in an effort to fill a faculty vacancy—compromises its purpose in an effort to upgrade the academic quality of the institution. Ask the recruiter about the hiring policy and whether or not new faculty and staff are required to sign a statement of faith. If the recruiter doesn't know, a quick call to the academic vice president's office can provide the information you are seeking.

2. Mission Statements and Goals

Watch this one carefully. My experience is that if you cannot find anything about a Christian experience in the mission statement or list of objectives, the school is not likely to be a truly Christian school. On the other hand, the mention of Christianity or God or faith in a mission statement doesn't necessarily mean it is a Christian campus. To you it should mean only that it makes the first cut in your sorting process.

Want some examples? I reviewed the mission statements of schools from various denominations. The examples below should give you some idea of what to look for during your own search. Also, pay attention to how differently each school talks about Christian beliefs, commitment, and heritage. I'm not familiar enough with these schools to offer a personal endorsement, but the variety of mission statements will show what you can expect to find in your own search.

Trinity Western University—Evangelical Free Church

The mission of Trinity Western University, as an arm of the church, is to develop godly Christian leaders: positive, goal-oriented university minds; growing disciples of Jesus Christ who glorify God through fulfilling the Great Commission, serving God and people in the marketplaces of life.

http://www.twu.ca/explore/explorMi.htm

Regent University Graduate School of Business— Nondenominational Charismatic

The School of Business participates fully in Regent University's vision to transform society through Christian leadership. For us, that vision means preparing men and women to build dynamic organizations that provide life-improving products and services in a way that points to the life-giver, Jesus Christ. Our distinctive is servant-leadership (Matthew 20:20–28). Our emphasis is preparing people to lead and manage people. Our context is the business world, including both profit and nonprofit organizations.

http://beacon.regent.edu/acad/schbus/header.html

81

Concordia University System—Missouri Synod Lutheran

Concordia University System will:

1. Witness the truth of the Gospel of Jesus Christ.
2. Offer an education wherein faith and learning are comprehensively integrated.
3. Provide a Lutheran Christian perspective for campus life and the academic programs.
4. Educate students of diverse ages and cultures for lives of service to church and community.
5. Be a partner in the Great Commission with other institutions and agencies of the Lutheran Church—Missouri Synod.

http://www.cus.edu

The College of St. Scholastica—Benedictine Catholic

The College of St. Scholastica is shaped by its Benedictine heritage. For more than fifteen hundred years Benedictines have cherished and promoted the importance of community, the uniqueness of the individual, the dignity of human labor, the worth of all human life, the beautiful and fitting in divine worship, the love of learning and the culture, stewardship in God's world, moderation in all aspects of life, with Benedictine educational institutions throughout the world.

http://www.css.edu/about/aboutmission.html

William Jewell College—American Baptist

To be an institution loyal to the ideals of Christ, demonstrating a Christian philosophy for the whole life and expressing the Missouri Baptist heritage which is the foundation of the College.

As a community in which the Christian commitment of the members exemplifies the compatibility of sound scholarship and the Christian faith in daily life, the College challenges the individual to embrace a value system advocating the caring relationships and social concern.

http://www.jewell.edu/pr/mission.htm

Whether we express our mission as "growing disciples of Jesus Christ" (Trinity Western University), through "servant-leadership" (Regent University), emphasize integration (Concordia), discuss "the beautiful and fitting in divine worship" (College of St. Scholastica), or express ourselves through "a Christian philosophy" (William Jewell College), all of these schools have one thing in common. Each school's mission statement expresses a unique Christian message.

All of this raises some valid questions: It's great that a school can write a mission statement reflecting Christian values and a focus on Jesus Christ, but when it comes to daily challenges, how successful are they at fulfilling their mission? And whose responsibility is it to ensure that an institution does what its mission claims it will do? Most schools are accredited by a nonreligious organization. Among other things, this organization is supposed to determine if a school's mission statement is being fulfilled. The bad news is that, in my experience, most secular accrediting organizations are not really equipped to determine if an institution is truly meeting its spiritual goals. These accreditation groups are masters at evaluating academic performance, but they struggle with how to evaluate the intricacies of a given doctrinal or spiritual persuasion.

Do the board of trustees, president, and alumni keep the school directed toward their mission? Some boards and administrations take the spiritual mission very seriously, and some alumni do not hesitate to write letters of encouragement or challenge regarding spiritual matters. Sadly, other boards of directors, administrators, and alumni get hung up on external issues, such as the presence or absence of dancing on campus. Their attention and energy are focused on these visible behaviors while the more substantive concern of the presence of God's message in the locker room, classroom, and residence hall is sometimes lost. The reason may be because the first is easier to evaluate than the second.

I guess I'm saying all this to make the point that the mission statement is a start but does not by itself tell the whole story of spiritual health of a campus. Once you find a school with a strong mission statement, don't be shy about asking the recruiter, faculty members, and students about how the goals of that statement are reflected in day-to-day campus events.

3. Chapel Programs

Although I'm sure it is possible to have a Christian college without the existence of chapel programs, they are a good indicator of the spiritual climate on campus. As I mentioned previously, a lot of information about an institution can be gained from the frequency and content of chapel programs. At Abilene Christian University, for example, students assemble daily for a thirty-minute chapel experience designed to encourage spiritual growth. In contrast, the closest thing to "chapel" on one Christian campus is a weekly forum in which a variety of religious and non-religious topics are presented. But the most common arrangement at the Christian schools I have visited is to offer chapel in the morning, two or three times a week for about one hour with required attendance.

Being comfortable with the frequency as well as the flavor of the worship experience is extremely important to school selection. There are too many college students who dread the chapel hour because they selected a school that offers the wrong type of worship experience for them. It may be a general lecture series instead of the praise and worship experience they expected, or possibly there is too much praise and worship and not enough biblical teaching.

Palm Beach Atlantic University provides a large public chapel format once a week. On other days there are chapel opportunities centered around themes. Here is an example of a spring semester chapel schedule at Palm Beach Atlantic.

General Chapel Sessions

PALM BEACH ATLANTIC UNIVERSITY

January 7	Dan Goodman
January 14	Carol Anderson and Jim Shores—Acts of Renewal
January 21	Truth
January 28	Dr. Eugene Hall, Provost

February 4	Rev. Gerald Kisner from Tabernacle Missionary Baptist Church, with David and Nicole Mullen
February 11	Worship Chapel with Dr. Marshall Truehill
February 18	Bruce Cripe with World Vision
March 4	Father Walter Dockerill from St. Rita Catholic Church
March 11–13	Staley Lectures with Dr. William Hendricks
March 18	Concert Choir
March 25	Senior Chapel
April 1	Founders Day
April 8	Awards Day
April 15	Summer Missions Commissioning

Extra Chapel Opportunities

Looking for Love Series

January 14	Love Addictions, 7 P.M.
January 16	Size 7 Forever, 10:30 A.M.
January 23	How to Have a Good Fight, 10:30 A.M.
January 30	What Eskimos Teach Us about Lust, 10:30 A.M.
February 6	Keys for Effective Dating, 10:30 A.M.

Real Life—Real Faith (All are at 10:30 A.M.)

March 20	Sanctioned Violence: Is There Anything Wrong with War, Capital Punishment, or Abortion?
March 27	Divided We Fall or Divide and Conquer? What's Right and What's Wrong with Having So Many Christian Denominations?
April 3	Paging Dr. Kevorkian: The Response of Faith to Assisted Suicide, Euthanasia, and Other Issues of Medical Ethics
April 10	Is the Internet Moral, Immoral, or Amoral? Interpreting the Role of Technology in the Community

Newman Club (All are at 10:30 A.M.)

| January 16 | Faith or Works |
| February 6 | Purgatory/Heaven/Hell/Devils/Angels/Grace |

February 20	Devotion to the Virgin Mary
March 6	Panel of Catholic Students, "How I Practice My Faith on a Daily Basis and How My Faith Affects My Career Choice"
March 20	The Sacraments
April 17	The Pope, Priests, and Nuns

Career Development Center (All held at 10:30 A.M.)

February 6	Finding Your Place in the World
March 6	Careers in Ministry I
April 3	Careers in Ministry II

Music and Fine Arts

March 21	Chamber Music Recital, 8 P.M.
April 4	PBA Symphony Concert, 8 P.M.
April 10	Women's Chorale/Handbells Concert, 8 P.M.
April 13	Concert Choir Spring Concert, 3 P.M.
April 14	Oratorio Chorus, Haydn's Creation, Bethesda-by-the-Sea

Institute for Faith and the Arts

March 11	Student Literature Night, 7:30 P.M.
March 12	Religion Colloquium, 7:30 P.M.
March 13	Student Art Night, 7:30 P.M.
March 15	Church Architecture Tour, 10 A.M.
March 27	Maundy Thursday Service

It's easy to see that a lot of thought has gone into offering many kinds of chapel experiences and opportunities for spiritual growth at this school!

Let me give you another example of a school that takes chapel seriously. At Azusa Pacific University, chapel is held three days a week. What is unusual about this school is that a variety of chapel services are held simultaneously at multiple sites on campus. Each site has its own worship team with a variety of formats, ranging from traditional to "free worship." The main speaker for the day is then electronically shown live on a large video screen at each satellite location on campus. In addition to this format, there is also a rather unique senior chapel called "Common Ground," where soon-to-be graduates set aside an hour on Tuesday nights to address their own unique issues and concerns through "speakers, worship and prayer."[1]

Another unique college chapel program is "Online Chapel" at Berean University. Here students or the general public can connect to a whole series of chapel activities on the World Wide Web at http://www.berean.edu/chapel/index.html. These activities include praise reports, prayer requests, daily devotions, a weekly chapel service through an audio feature, or interaction with a prayer partner—all online. In fact, this whole university experience is handled online. While I cannot speak to the quality of this program, it provides a very innovative option for those whose schedule doesn't allow them to attend a traditional university.

4. Prayer Ministry

A good indicator of a Christian university is the presence of a prayer ministry. Don't confuse a prayer ministry with prayer towers and prayer chapels. Buildings like these may reflect the interests of a well-intentioned donor who specifically designated such a building, rather than the interests of the campus.

Some campuses have informal prayer groups, while other schools have much more formal programs. The Intercessory Prayer Ministry at Dallas Baptist University is comprised of a full-time director, several student workers, a daily e-mail prayer system, a prayer network of more than twelve hundred senior citizens who have committed themselves to praying for university needs, and a prayer room manned by DBU faculty and staff who volunteer—for fifteen-minute increments throughout the day—to pray for community requests.

5. Special Campus Events and Ministries

A review of special events can be a good indicator of the spiritual environment on campus. Sometimes this information is printed on a campus calendar that is available by request, or it may be online on the computer Web page for the institution. For example, here are some of the ministries available at two institutions. Based on the ministries offered, it's not difficult to discern what is important on these campuses.

Spring Arbor College

On-Campus Ministries

1. Walk through the Bible—A weekend seminar once each semester, dealing with the importance of the Bible in life
2. Celebration—A Wednesday night meeting consisting of prayer, worship, and Bible study
3. Spiritual Life Retreat—A weekend excursion in October, full of biblical teaching and relaxation at Yankee Springs State Park
4. Collegians for Life—A student branch of the Right to Life organization
5. S.W.A.T. (Students with a Testimony)—A Bible study dealing with practical ways of sharing the gospel
6. Blood Drive—A very practical ministry of donating life through the Red Cross, once each semester
7. Skip-a-Meal—A chance for students to give up a meal and let the proceeds assist in feeding the hungry
8. Reflection Groups—A ministry of fellowship, accountability, prayer, and Bible study in groups of five to ten people meeting weekly

Off-Campus Ministries

1. Arbor Manor—A weekly ministry of compassion to the residents of the local nursing care center
2. Action Jackson—A weekly outreach to the inner-city children and families of Jackson
3. Men's Prison—A weekly worship service held in the SPSM men's facility in Jackson

4. Navajo Nation—A spring-break service trip, ministering to Navajo people through the Navajo mission in Farmington, New Mexico
5. Interfaith Shelter—A service-oriented ministry to the homeless of Jackson, involving fellowship and serving food
6. Women's Prison—A monthly Bible study held in the Florence Crane women's facility in Coldwater
7. NYC—A service and evangelism–oriented spring-break trip, ministering in the heart of New York City
8. Homefront—A spring-break service and ministry trip, working with existing ministries in the state of Michigan

http://www.arbor.edu/campuslf/stuserv/stumin.htm

Westmont College

On-Campus Ministries

1. Abstinence—A support group for students seeking to maintain purity in their sexual lives
2. Areopagus—A support group for Christian students grappling with difficult questions and doubts about their faith
3. Barnabas—A support group that provides encouragement through special attention, surprises, and prayer to those on campus who are in times of special need
4. Bible Study and Fellowship Groups—Available for students to spend time studying Scripture and sharing life's struggles and joys with each other
5. Prayer Warriors—A group of students who gather together to pray, especially for the needs of the Westmont community
6. Vespers—A weekly Sunday night gathering of students for the purpose of worship, prayer, and community sharing

Off-Campus Ministries

1. Adopt-a-Grandparent—A ministry to the elderly throughout Santa Barbara nursing homes through visitation, sharing, and encouragement
2. Amigos—A ministry to the Hispanic community through teaching English as a second language

3. Casa Rosa—A ministry with recovering drug- or alcohol-addicted mothers and their children under the age of five, providing babysitting while mothers attend meetings
4. Colors of Christ—A ministry to spread joy and happiness in the name of Christ to children, the handicapped, and the elderly through the use of mime and clowning
5. Habitat for Humanity—Helps to build and improve homes for the needy
6. Homeless Ministry—A ministry committed to working with, understanding, and loving the homeless population of Santa Barbara, through visitation and prayer
7. Juvenile Hall—A ministry to the struggling youth in juvenile hall by building friendships and providing good role models
8. Reach Out—A one-day event when students reach out through various nonprofit organizations in the Santa Barbara area to provide needed services, such as painting, gardening, moving, cleaning, and washing windows
9. Sidewalk Sunday School—A ministry to the minority children of Santa Barbara for a couple of hours every Sunday through games, crafts, and Bible studies

http://www.westmont.edu/StudentLife/offcampus.html

Other Ministries

In addition to opportunities like these, many schools offer global ministry events that involve traveling to other countries, such as the Tri-S (Student Summer Service) program at my alma mater, Anderson University. Each year about five hundred young people (out of the two thousand students who attend this college) volunteer to build, repair, paint, teach, counsel, research, sing, or provide nursing service in places like Africa, Australia, Asia, Europe, Latin America, and the Caribbean. Dozens of work teams visit different parts of the world—often linking up with missionaries—and make a profound difference in people's lives. During these experiences, students work and often live with nationals, developing a real global view firsthand.

It would be hard to imagine that anyone with an interest in ministry could not find somewhere to get involved on one of these campuses. You may wish to use these lists as a yardstick with which to compare a school of your choosing, to help you evaluate how focused that school is on ministry. College is a great time to begin a lifetime of service by working on teams like these. Don't miss the importance of these ministries in your college selection, because they can easily be as critical to your education as the classroom experiences.

I have long forgotten much of what I was taught in my undergraduate classes, but I will never forget trying to sing Christian songs (I can't sing, maybe that's why I remember it so well) and share the gospel on the streets of Arhus, Denmark, as a part of Anderson University's Tri-S program. I don't know if anyone we witnessed to was positively affected (a few people threw vegetables at us, and eventually the police asked us to move on) but I can tell you that this strengthened my faith and gave me an appreciation for street witnessing. Other ministry experiences I had at Anderson University—riding a bicycle through Europe, teaching English in Japan, and remodeling a building on a Navajo Reservation—are primarily responsible for the global interests and sensitivity that I cherish today.

While students, faculty, and staff at ministry-minded schools, such as Spring Arbor, Westmont, and Anderson, are to be commended for great opportunities they offer both on and off campus, the good news is that there are many other Christian colleges and universities across the country with similar programs. And if you can't find the ministry you feel called to support, you may want to start your own group. While he was still a college student, Dr. Gary Cook, president at Dallas Baptist University, recognized the need for a campus ministry of Habitat for Humanity. (Habitat for Humanity is an organization that refurbishes older homes or builds new ones for families that cannot otherwise afford to remodel or buy their own home.) As a result of Cook's concern, he formed the first campus chapter long before he became a college president. Today there are chapters all over the country.

6. Integration of Faith and Learning

One major distinguishing characteristic among Christian colleges is how classes outside the area of religion are taught. I believe that you cannot separate your faith from your education or ultimately from your vocation. If you believe that a Christian's mission on earth is to spread the good news about Jesus Christ, then it follows that while Christians may choose different courses of study in college, we all have the same objectives. The goal of a Christian education is to illustrate how God works in each subject area. We call this marriage of our Christian beliefs with our education the "integration of faith and learning."

I'm going to give you a little quiz to see if you know what I'm talking about since you're looking a little bored with all of this. Here are several classroom situations. Put a check beside the ones where integration of faith and learning are taking place.

Integration Quiz

_____1. A student in math class reads a devotional that relates to a problem he is having at home.

_____2. Your history teacher takes prayer requests and then begins class with a prayer.

_____3. The last day of class your economics teacher gives his personal testimony.

_____4. Your biology teacher demonstrates how creation theory fits biblical truths.

_____5. A speaker in chapel outlines the journeys of Paul.

Now grade yourself. The only example of true integration is number 4. If you got five out of five correct, go to your parents and tell them they owe you a trip to the Bahamas. If you got four or less right, you have to continue reading this book. Seriously, while I would encourage all of these religious activities in a Christian university, the only one that brings together faith and the content area of the discipline is the biology teacher discussing creation theory.

Let me give you another example of the integration of faith and learning. When I teach Business Management and Organization in the business school, I ask my students to read the biblical book of Nehemiah from the standpoint of Nehemiah being a middle manager. Then, as a class, we go through each chapter and talk about management principles that can be taken from this Old Testament account.

From this vantage point, one of the chapters of Nehemiah takes on great significance. I know you probably have Nehemiah memorized, but in case you don't, chapter three lists in great detail the various families, tribes, and ethnic groups that rebuilt each section of the walls of Jerusalem. Boring, right? Not from a management point of view! In this passage, we learn how Nehemiah was able to work with a variety of ethnic groups and get them collectively working on a common goal. What manager doesn't need this skill today?

Second, Nehemiah asked workers to build the wall in the area closest to their house: Can you think of a better motivation for quality control than to have people making sure the enemy didn't break through the part of the wall closest to their family?

And finally, of all the people mentioned in this chapter, the first is Eliashib, the high priest who rebuilt the Sheep Gate. Even though I cannot tell you much about the Sheep Gate, I can tell you how significant it was to have an opinion leader like the high priest—who under normal circumstances probably did very little manual labor—out in front of everybody, building a gate. I don't think this was done by accident. Anyway, in the process of studying this chapter, we are able to illustrate how the Bible can be used as a manual for managers.

Unfortunately, many Christian universities either do not embrace this concept of integration or don't understand it. On some Christian campuses there is considerable effort invested in devotional times and spiritual experiences, but these experiences don't often impact course content. Many faculty don't have a good understanding of how to integrate faith into their course material because the vast majority of master's and doctoral degrees are awarded at secular universities where this concept would not be taught. Therefore, unless the Christian university trains its faculty to integrate their faith and their academic discipline and to include this integration in their teaching, it probably won't be done. I commend institutions that spend considerable time with their faculty in workshops and orientation sessions, wrestling with how they can best convey to the student the relationship between faith and knowledge.

If you are looking for a college or university that actively pursues the integration of faith with learning, here are some suggestions as to how you may identify such a school:

Look for this concept mentioned in any of the catalogs or materials from the school.

This will not always answer the question as this concept is not always discussed in promotional materials. Some research should indicate where integration of faith with learning is a fundamental part of the educational experience.

The following are quotations found on the Web pages of various Christian colleges. In each one I have italicized the words that support the concept of integration.

Wheaton College states:

. . . the Department of Education seeks to prepare prospective teachers to *integrate* Christian values and ethical practices in the educational setting, through an understanding that each student is uniquely created by God in his image and by demonstrating Christian integrity and moral behavior.

http://www.wheaton.edu/EducHome.html

Mars Hill College states:

. . . Mars Hill emphasizes the values of our faith, and we believe this provides an open supportive environment for learning, personal growth, and moral maturity. At Mars Hill, students are challenged to *integrate faith with facts,* and to discover practical applications to strengthen commitment.

http://www.mhc.edu/intro/text/spirit.htm

Geneva College states:

In Christian education the curriculum is built upon the thesis that the historic Christian faith is permanently true, and that it is the *integrating* factor of a truly Christian educational program. Since

Christian education leads toward an understanding of God, man, and the universe in their interrelatedness, the curriculum will have a strong emphasis on both the Humanities and the Sciences, theoretic and applied, as well as a basic core of Biblical studies. The curriculum should lead a person to grasp the foundations of learning so that he can live a life glorifying to God, confronting honestly and confidently the problems and challenges of new knowledge, and contributing to the welfare of society under God.

http://www.geneva.edu/concepts.html

Wayland Baptist University states that in its business school the student receives:

Real world application
Academic excellence
Professionally qualified faculty
Integration of faith and learning
Enhanced career potential
Commitment to quality

http://www.texasonline.net/wbu/body.htm

While the format of expression is very different at each of these schools, the idea of integration is evident.

Ask students during your campus visit whether the instructors introduce religious concepts in the content of their lectures.
I would avoid using the phrase "integration of faith with learning" because students may not be familiar with the concept. Keep in mind that methods of integration are as varied as the number of instructors on a college campus because how one relates his or her faith to the content of a course is a very personal experience, just as our faith is a personal relationship with God.

Interview an instructor in your field of study and ask how he or she integrates faith into the course.
My experience is that some instructors will stumble a little on this question and others will come alive and give you more than you really wanted to know.

I realize this integration stuff may sound very boring, but, believe me, if you attend a school where it's being done, it will make a big difference in your education.

7. Membership in the Coalition for Christian Colleges and Universities

While there are strong Christian schools that are not members of CCCU, affiliation with this organization means a lot. CCCU is an association of more than ninety schools located across the United States and Canada. Some of these schools are nondenominational in nature and others are affiliated with specific denominations. For a full listing of these schools and links to their Internet home pages, check http://www.gospelcom.net/cgi-bin /cccu_alpha/.

If you would prefer to access this information in a book format, Peterson's *Choose a Christian College* contains a listing of each of these Coalition schools along with a one-page description of each.[2] The Peterson's guide is particularly helpful if you want to compare general data regarding schools. For example, if you are looking for a Christian school with more than two thousand students that has an intercollegiate volleyball team and offers a major in physical therapy, in the Peterson's guide you can quickly determine that Azusa Pacific and Southwest Baptist University meet your requirements.

To become a member of CCCU, a university must meet the following criteria:

1. Primary orientation as a four-year college or university in North America with curriculum rooted in the arts and sciences. U.S. institutions must have full nonprobationary regional accreditation.
2. A public mission based upon the centrality of Jesus Christ and evidence of how faith is integrated with the institution's academic and student life programs.
3. A current hiring policy that requires of each full-time faculty member and administrator a personal faith in Jesus Christ.

4. A commitment to advancing the cause of Christian higher education through active participation in the programs of the Coalition, payment of the annual dues and special assessments, and institutional practices that have been, are now, and will continue to be supportive of other Coalition members.
5. Institutional fund-raising activities which are consistent with the standards of the Evangelical Council for Financial Accountability and demonstration of responsible financial operations.

While there is some variance, as might be expected, in the quality of education among the ninety plus schools and there are good Christian universities that do not belong to this group, these five membership criteria from CCCU go a long way in establishing a good starting point for a Christian college search. For more information, write Coalition for Christian Colleges and Universities at 329 Eighth Street, NE, Washington, D.C. 20002-6158; 202-546-8713; fax 202-546-8913; Web site http://www.cccu.org.

The Coalition also offers high-quality Christian programs that would not be financially possible for one school alone to provide. Imagine yourself spending a semester taking classes in Egypt, England, Russia, China, Costa Rica, Hollywood, or Washington, D.C., earning credits toward your college degree. I have talked to more than thirty of my students about these programs over the years and they always say they were stretched, worked very hard, and would do it again in a minute. If you are interested in more information on any of these programs, I have compiled a brief description of each program from the Internet.

American Studies Program (http://www.gospelcom.net/cccu/students/asp.html). Students spend a semester in Washington, D.C., studying domestic and international public policy issues and serving in internships.

China Studies Program. Students interested in China will have the opportunity to engage this intriguing country from the inside. The semester will include study of standard Chinese language, geography, history, religion, culture, and China's modern development (available January 1999).

Latin American Studies Program (http://www.gospelcom.net/cccu/students/lasp.html). Based in San Jose, Costa Rica, this semester-long program combines study of Latin American politics, economics, religion, language, and culture with travel and a service project.

Los Angeles Film Studies Center (http://www.gospelcom.net/cccu/students/lafsc.html). The LAFSC provides students with the opportunity to explore the film industry and film's impact on culture from a liberal arts perspective and to serve in an internship in the industry.

Middle East Studies Program (http://www.gospelcom.net/cccu/students/mesp.html). Based in Cairo, Egypt, the MESP examines the history, language, cultures, religious life, and the political and economic dimensions of the region.

Oxford Honors Program. Junior and senior honors students will have the opportunity to study in England by participating in an interdisciplinary semester in Oxford through a partnership program with the Centre for Medieval and Renaissance Studies, affiliated with Keble College of the University of Oxford (available Fall 1998).

Russian Studies Program (http://www.gospelcom.net/cccu/students/rsp.html). RSP students experience life in three Russian cities while studying the country's language, history, culture, and politics.

Summer programs are also available for the Oxford Honors Program and the Summer Institute of Journalism in Washington, D.C.

8. Participation in the Focus on the Family Institute

Another strong educational program with which many fine Christian schools are affiliated is the Focus on the Family Institute. Similar in many ways to the educational programs offered by the Coalition for Christian Colleges, the Family Institute provides a unique educational experience which prepares young leaders to develop a Christian worldview regarding family and society. This program—offered at the Focus on the Family headquarters in Colorado Springs, Colorado—affirms traditional values such as the importance of fatherhood, two-parent families, marital fidelity, parental authority, and faith in God.

The Family Institute provides both summer and traditional semester programs offering the following types of courses:
Marriage, Parenting and Leadership
The Sanctity of Family Life
Contemporary Thought and Culture
Government and Social Policy
The semester-long program also contains a practicum experience at Focus on the Family or within the surrounding community, and a lecture from a nationally prominent leader. For more information, contact:

Focus on the Family Institute
8605 Explorer Drive
Colorado Springs, CO 80920
Phone (719) 531-5181
FAX (719) 548-4666
Web Site: http://www.family.org/welcome/aboutfof/
A0000080.html

Summary

While many good colleges and universities may not have all the characteristics mentioned in this chapter, the more they possess of them, the more likely they are to offer a truly Christ-centered environment. A mission statement that clearly identifies a strong spiritual purpose, regular chapel services with true worship experiences, a wide range of active ministries offered on and off campus, affiliations with other Christian colleges and associations, prayer ministries, a commitment to have a Christian faculty, and an emphasis on integration of faith and learning are all signs of a Christian campus.

You probably won't find a convenient listing of "truly Christian schools" in the college guide sitting on the desk of your high school guidance counselor. Locating schools that value the spiritual health of their students will take a little planning and effort on your part, but let me assure you that there are outstanding Christian institutions in virtually every part of the country that meet these criteria (see appendix B for a partial listing).

99

8

When a Secular University Is the Best Choice

How to Live Out Your Faith in Any Setting

Brent Mathis always knew what he wanted to do when he grew up. In grade school, while other students were still coloring outside the lines of their coloring books, Brent was using his straight edge to put the finishing touches on his drawing of a three-story dog house. (I could use a design like that for those days I get in trouble with my wife.) By junior high Brent had mastered the drafting program on his computer and in high school had made serious designs for a 5,000-square-foot home.

When it came time to go to college, Brent began what seemed like mission impossible to find a Christian university offering a degree in the area of architecture he wanted to study. Discouraged, Brent thought he was settling for less than the best in his local public university, but to his surprise Brent found several Christian groups on campus, and they made his college years a time of growth in every way.

While I am a firm believer in Christian universities and am a proud alumnus of Anderson University in Anderson, Indiana, I have also received two degrees from a public university and am very thankful for this education as well. Possibly you need to stay close to home to take care of family obligations, or maybe you don't have the money to go to a Christian university. Maybe you just believe a secular university will give you a better education in your particular field or you feel that God is calling you to ministry as a student in a secular university.

Christian Student Groups

Regardless of the reason you are considering a secular institution, it is important to know that God's presence and purpose can be found at any school. In fact, godly fellowship, sound biblical guidance, and the presence of God's own Holy Spirit can be experienced through Bible studies and prayer meetings on virtually any campus.

Now let's be honest with each other for a moment. When you read the words "Bible studies" and "prayer meetings," did you get an image of a group of silver-haired folk memorizing "the begats" or requesting prayer for bad backs and dying friends? If so, you are in for a pleasant surprise, because some of the most together and alive ministries in existence today are on secular college campuses. In the following pages, I will introduce you to some outstanding Christian groups, designed to help you grow spiritually and enjoy godly fellowship as you pursue your education.

InterVarsity Christian Fellowship

InterVarsity is a nondenominational Christian group dedicated to encouraging students to hold each other accountable and pointed toward the hope of Jesus Christ. "The vision of InterVarsity Christian Fellowship is to build collegiate fellowships, develop disciples who embody biblical values, and engage the campus in all its ethnic diversity with the gospel of Jesus Christ."[1]

101

InterVarsity offers chapter meetings called Large Group meetings that provide "warm fellowship, worship and biblical teaching from local ministers, faculty, InterVarsity staff, and community people." This is the most visible of the activities on most campuses and likely the first event of this group you will experience on campus.

InterVarsity also promotes small-group (five to ten students) Bible studies that meet weekly for about an hour, and they also periodically sponsor prayer meetings focused on student needs. (Don't panic, the prayer meetings usually only last about thirty minutes.) Most InterVarsity groups also encourage students to share their faith, and they provide a variety of strategies and opportunities for this to happen. Finally, there are some great social events where you can meet other Christians. For example, in the first week of school at the University of Maryland, College Park, InterVarsity hosted the following events:

Weekly Bulletin

Capture the Campus/Water Balloon Fight	Friday 7 P.M.
Tailgate Party	Saturday 4:30 P.M.
Jerry's Pizza Party—Free Pizza for Newcomers!	Wednesday 7 P.M.
First Large Group	Thursday 7:30 P.M.
Crab Feast!	Friday 7 P.M.

I don't know about you, but the free pizza caught my attention! Seriously, there are plenty of great opportunities for quality fellowship with this group.

Contact InterVarsity Christian Fellowship at P.O. Box 7895, Madison, WI 53707-7895; http://www.cen.uiuc.edu.

The Navigators

The Navigators was founded in the 1930s by Dawson Trotman to meet a need for the military. Eventually spreading to colleges and universities, The Navigators fosters individual spiritual growth and provides skills and training in helping others know the Lord.

The Navigators has large-group meetings sometimes known as NAVS, supplemented by Bible studies and praise and worship programs. The chapter at San Diego State University, for example, has a NAVS meeting every Wednesday at 5:30 P.M. Students are encouraged to bring their meal and stay for Christian fellowship followed by a Bible study. One morning a week students meet at the United Campus Ministries building for an informal hour of praise and worship. A random week's activities with The Navigators at San Diego State included the following.[2]

NAVS Meeting and Bible Study	Wednesday
Ultimate Frisbee	Thursday
Fun Game/Movie Night	Saturday

Contact The Navigators at P.O. Box 6000, Colorado Springs, CO 80934; http://www.gospelcom.net/navs/.

Campus Crusade for Christ International

Started in 1951 by Dr. Bill Bright while he was a student at Fuller Theological Seminary, Campus Crusade is a nondenominational, international Christian ministry with a mission to "turn lost students and believers into Christ-centered laborers." Today there are an estimated 11,800 full-time and 32,000 associate staff serving in 150 countries in an attempt to reach the world for Christ.

The vision of Campus Crusade is described as follows:

- See that every student from every social and ethnic culture has an opportunity to hear the gospel in a manner that relates to his or her life experience, while giving an opportunity to respond to Christ.
- See those who put their faith in Christ nurtured in that new relationship with an opportunity to grow in the context of a healthy spiritual family.
- See students go to the ends of the earth to minister to others and declare the good news of the gospel.[3]

At the University of Colorado, for example, Campus Crusade members meet every Thursday night at 7:30 P.M. as a large group for singing, fellowship, and teaching. During the semester, there are small-group Bible studies scattered across campus along with social events and days of training and outreach.

On the Internet, Campus Crusade provides a "Campus Locator Map," showing campuses that have Campus Crusade ministries. Another tool available is "Leadership U," a virtual campus that helps people with common interests and missions link up with resources from various campuses.

Contact Campus Crusade for Christ International at 100 Sunport Lane, Orlando, FL 32809; http://www.cci.org/.

Christian Leadership Ministries

A ministry of Campus Crusade for Christ International, Christian Leadership Ministries is a network of more than ten thousand Christian professors from more than seven hundred universities dedicated to providing a nationwide Christian outreach to college and university professors. This unique ministry includes both faculty and students teamed together in a popular outreach called Favorite Faculty Banquets. At these banquets, students share their appreciation for their favorite professors, and then a carefully chosen keynote speaker communicates the message of Jesus Christ. On many campuses Christian faculty speak about their faith as it relates to their discipline in a series of lectures called the Faculty Forum. This group is an excellent resource for students who wish to find a Christian perspective or mentor on a secular campus.

Contact Christian Leadership Ministries at P.O. Box 790609, Dallas, TX 75379-0609.

Baptist Student Union

The first Baptist Student Union (BSU) group I came across on the Internet was at Arizona State University (http://w3.arizona.edu/~bsu/others.html). Lots of details and a clear map to direct students to the BSU building were given. Even an advertisement for the low price of a Coke in the BSU vending machine ($.40) was part of the critical information I was able to find.

One of the key BSU events at Arizona State University is Club 901, which takes place every Friday night at 6 P.M. Students who attend are treated to free home-cooked meals. Free food always gets my attention as long as it isn't stuff that is "good for you." Oh yeah, I got so excited about the free food that I almost forgot that they have music, drama, and inspirational teaching as well. Below is the schedule of evening programs for Club 901 for one fall semester.[4]

August 23	First Club 901 of the year!!!
August 30	Authenticity
September 6	Healthy Friendships
September 13	Truth Telling in Relationships
September 20	Patagonia Retreat
September 27	Dealing with Failure
October 4	Forgiveness
October 11	World Hunger
October 19	Missions Dessert (no Club 901)
October 25	Helplessness/Depression
November 1	Emotional Healing from Abuse
November 6	Ministering to "Generation X"
November 15	The Post-Modern Mind-set
November 22	Dating
November 29	THANKSGIVING BREAK!!!

I just wish they had said what they are serving for dinner . . .

Arizona State's BSU home page also gave a list of thirty-six other BSU home pages at schools across the country with equally great programs. Don't assume that because a school you are interested in is not listed on the Internet it doesn't have a BSU program.

Contact Baptist Student Union at National Student Ministry Division, Baptist Sunday School Board, 127 Ninth Avenue North, Nashville, TN 37234; http://www.bgct.org/.

Christian Campus Organizations and Related Churches

Let's say for a moment that your prospective campus doesn't have The Navigators, InterVarsity, Campus Crusade, Baptist Student Union, or any other Christian group. What now? One of the best ways to find a good local group is to check the directory of the university for religious organizations. You can do this by calling the campus operator or looking up the university on the Internet. You may be surprised what you can find out about these campus groups and church groups in the area even before you visit the campus or make your college choice.

To see what I could find, I randomly picked four universities from around the country—Drexel University, Penn State University, University of Colorado at Boulder, and University of California at Santa Barbara—and launched my own search for Christian groups. I have no contacts or friends at any of these campuses, so I had no idea what I would find.

At Drexel University in Philadelphia I found an Interfaith Council, which included a group called Asbury Protestant Ministries under the leadership of Rev. Tim Thomson-Hohl, an ordained United Methodist minister. His phone number was given for contact by interested students or parents. Asbury Ministries is an ecumenical campus ministry seeking to provide spiritual presence, pastoral guidance, and a prophetic voice. This is accomplished through small sharing groups, pastoral counseling, lectures, and workshops.

With a little research of Penn State I found a good resource in the office of the chaplain under the direction of Rev. Will Gipson. The chaplain's office works with several groups of different faiths; however, three that might be of most interest to a Christian in search of fellowship were Christian Association, Newman Center for Roman Catholic Students, and Orthodox Christian Fellowship.

A search on the Internet through the University of Colorado, Boulder, home page produced a list of churches from which I selected two to review in more detail. The first, Atonement Lutheran Church, had a home page on the Internet where I was able to review the church's weekly activities and determine, for example, that they were very involved in supporting groups like Habitat for Humanity. If there was any concern about the church's theology, the prior week's sermon was available online for careful review. In less than fifteen minutes, I knew more about this church than many of its neighbors did, even though I was several hundred miles away.

The second church I reviewed from the campus list was Boulder Mennonite Church, which among a series of other ministries has a group called BMC Care Groups. These groups would be of particular interest to students looking for a small group of Christian friends with twelve or fewer members. Care groups are the key pastoral structure of this church with the leaders being trained and supervised by church pastors. At the time of my search, these groups met the second and fourth Sunday evenings of each month. Even the distinctives of these care groups was available via Internet, so visitors could find out about the groups before attending. Here are some of the distinctives:

Groups agree to confidentiality. Nobody criticizes behind another's back.

Group members listen to and care for each other. They pray for each other and help each other in times of need.

Group leaders meet with each other and the pastor monthly for supervision and continuing education.

The topics of discussion for each period are also available on the Internet. Topics ranged from examining racism to a spiritual look at creativity. Sign me up!

The last school I researched was University of California at Santa Barbara. One of the unique ministries I found there was a series of Christian seminars being conducted on this campus by Christian faculty and guests. That's right, Christian seminars on a public campus! All seminars are presented during lunch on Tuesdays in the University Center. Seminars for the fall quarter are listed on the next page to give some idea of the type of session that could be expected on one state university campus:

October 1: "Christianity after the USSR: Some Personal Experiences," Steve McLean, Professor of Mechanical and Environmental Engineering

October 8: "Looking East: A Protestant and Eastern Orthodoxy," Rev. Josiah Trenham, St. Athanasius

October 15: "Imitating Jesus: Learning to Become Like Him," Ron Smith, Turnpike Church of Christ

October 22: "C. S. Lewis," Reed Jolly

October 29: "Christians and Muslims in Bosnia: The Hope of Reconciliation," Dan Philpott, Assistant Professor of Political Science, UCSB

November 5: "The State of the University," Frank Hensley, Christian Leadership Ministries

November 12: "Persecution and Tolerance in Medieval Christianity," Carol Lansing, Associate Professor of History, UCSB

November 19: "Implications of Quantum Theory for Christian Theology," Bob Griffiths, visiting researcher, Institute for Theoretical Physics, UCSB

November 26: "Incarnation and Images of the Nativity of Christ," Rev. Ed Nowak, St. Mark's University Parish

I hate to admit it, but the concept of quantum theory impacting theology might be a little over my head. Can you relate? I want you to know, however, that despite my lack of mental gymnastics, even we boneheads can appreciate the fact that these topics do demonstrate a sharing of academic disciplines with faith, which would rival discussions on any Christian campus.

Christian Faculty and Staff

This chapter is by no means meant to be an exhaustive list of campus ministries nationwide or even on the campuses mentioned. I simply mention a few of these ministries to help students realize that there are strong, active Christian groups on secular campuses. In my research to date, I have yet to run across a campus where I could not find active Christian groups on or close to campus. And I don't even have to travel to campus to find this information! To my surprise, almost every university home page I have researched has led me, within minutes, to Christian groups. So despite all the challenges to your faith that there may be on secular campuses, the good news is that there are Christian support groups there too.

When you arrive on your secular campus, search out the Christian faculty. On many campuses at least once a year Christian faculty and staff publish their names in a campus advertisement to identify themselves. If you have trouble locating these faculty, try contacting one of the campus ministries mentioned previously or a local church. They may be able to direct you to faculty who are in their congregation. If you locate one Christian faculty member, it is likely that he or she will know others on campus. Their referral can help you identify faculty you wish to meet and ultimately consider as teachers or mentors. Christian professors can be an encouragement to you in many areas. They will probably know which class sections in your major are taught by fellow believers. Taking classes from a Christian can sometimes make all the difference in how the class goes for you.

9

College Accreditation

What Does It Mean to Me?

Old Mother Hubbard,
She left her cupboard
To get a college degree,
But when she got there,
The degree went nowhere,
So instead she watched MTV . . .

Every month I hear from students who are angry because they have attended college for two years and have just discovered that their course work will not transfer to any other school. Or, even worse, they have spent the past four years obtaining an under-graduate degree with the hope of pursuing a master's or doctor-ate and are finding they will not be accepted into any respectable graduate program in the country because their undergraduate "degree" is not considered valid. I have even interviewed would-be faculty members who did not realize, when they handed me their résumé, that because of the school from which they received their degree, I could never seriously consider them for a teaching position.

What's the big deal? Aren't all schools created equal?

Not exactly.

Degree Mills

Let's take an extreme case. In education circles, there are schools that are not-so-affectionately called "degree mills." In a worst-case scenario, you can send them a check for x amount of dollars, and they will send you back a diploma, no questions asked. But most degree mills aren't quite this blatant; they will try to pass themselves off as legitimate institutions, even letting you take a few classes by mail. Now not all correspondence courses are offered by degree mills, but most degree mills do operate through the mail.

Be wary of any school that wants money from you up front while doing very little admissions processing. Look for suspicious signs, such as an address that is a P.O. box or a personal residence, no phone number, misspelled words in the promotional materials, or the lack of a campus that you can visit. These may indicate that the organization will be in business only temporarily.

Be cautious when promotional efforts for a school you've never heard of are done over the phone.

Sadly, some con artists know that a casually mentioned statement about Christianity can cause real believers to lower their guard. A July 26, 1996, article in the *Chronicle of Higher Education* titled "FBI Agents Raid Correspondence School" cited a Louisiana man who granted degrees to thousands through an unaccredited "Christian" university correspondence program.[1] The owner, Mr. Kirk, operated LaSalle University of Louisiana as a nonprofit corporation founded by the World Wide Church. This "church" was formed with Mr. Kirk as president to shield it from review by the government. LaSalle University claimed to be accredited by the Council on Postsecondary Christian Education in Washington, D.C. But response to a call to the Council was only a prerecorded message, which referred callers to a toll-free number, which rang back at LaSalle University. Hello! Are we starting to get the picture here? The saddest part of the story is that this man used his claim of Christianity to take advantage of an estimated six thousand victims.

I wish I had a list of known degree mills and could warn you, "Don't apply to any of these schools!" Unfortunately this kind of list does not exist, because these "colleges" go out of business so quickly and then reappear under new names. A few sources, however, that may help you distinguish legitimate from fraudulent offers are:

National Fraud Center, 800-876-7060
Better Business Bureau, 703-525-8277
U.S. Office of Consumer Affairs, 202-395-7900
Postal Crime Hotline, 800-654-8896

The Importance of Accreditation

Another way to sort legitimate institutions from riffraff has to do with understanding something called accreditation. Accrediting bodies were formed to protect the public from scam artists in the education business and to assure that an institution meets a minimum standard. Accrediting groups send evaluators to campus to interview faculty and administrators and to review curriculum. They examine the qualifications of professors, library resources that are available to students, and the number of credit hours required for receiving a degree. If an institution meets the accrediting group's criteria, it receives accreditation, which is a stamp of approval, so to speak—a promise to the consumer that a certain standard of excellence has been met.

While there are many good schools without legitimate accreditation, the absence of key accreditation should be considered a serious warning sign in a college search. As I indicated at the beginning of this chapter, a degree from a nonaccredited school may make it impossible to be accepted at a graduate school or in landing some types of jobs.

I wish I could tell you that there is one accrediting group and that if any college meets the standards of this one group, it is a good place to receive an education. But the truth is that there are literally hundreds of accrediting groups, each with their own set of standards.

Regional Accreditation Associations

To simplify things, let me say here that the most important accreditation for a college or university is called a regional accreditation. A university that is regionally accredited must complete an extensive self-evaluation every ten years. Rather than having every school in the United States answer to a single national accreditation group, there are actually six regional accreditation groups across the country that make up an accreditation network. These six groups are listed below, with the states in which they have jurisdiction, their addresses, and their phone numbers. If you are unclear about whether or not the school you want to attend is regionally accredited, call the regional headquarters for the state in which the school is located.

Middle States Association of Colleges and Schools
Delaware, District of Columbia, Maryland, New Jersey, New York, Pennsylvania, Puerto Rico, Virgin Islands
Dr. Howard L. Simmons, executive director
Commission on Higher Education
3624 Market Street
Philadelphia, PA 19104
215-662-5606

New England Association of Schools and Colleges
Connecticut, Maine, Massachusetts, New Hampshire, Rhode Island, Vermont
Charles M. Cook, director
209 Burlington Road
Bedford, MA 01730-1433
617-271-0022, fax 617-271-0950

113

North Central Association of Colleges and Schools, Commission Institutions of Higher Education

Arizona, Arkansas, Colorado, Illinois, Indiana, Iowa, Kansas, Michigan, Minnesota, Missouri, Nebraska, New Mexico, North Dakota, Ohio, Oklahoma, South Dakota, West Virginia, Wisconsin, Wyoming

Dr. Patricia Thrash, executive director

159 N. Dearborn Street

Chicago, IL 60601

312-263-0456

Northwest Association of Schools and Colleges, Commission on Colleges

Alaska, Idaho, Montana, Nevada, Oregon, Utah, Washington

Dr. Joseph A. Milik, executive director

3700-B University Way, N.E.

Seattle, WA 98105

206-543-0195, fax 206-685-4621

Southern Association of Colleges and Schools

Alabama, Florida, Georgia, Kentucky, Louisiana, Mississippi, North Carolina, South Carolina, Tennessee, Texas, Virginia

James Rogers, executive director

1866 Southern Lane

Decatur, GA 30365

404-679-4500, 800-248-7701, fax 404-679-4558

Western Association of Schools and Colleges

California, Guam, Hawaii

Dr. John C. Peterson, executive director

Accrediting Commission for Senior Colleges and Universities

3060 Valencia Avenue, Suite 3

Aptos, CA 95003

510-632-5000

At the risk of repeating myself, let me say that while there are some excellent schools that for various reasons are not accredited, my advice is that you should find a regionally accredited institution for your education.

Biblical Christian Accreditation Groups

In addition to regional accreditations there are several specialty accreditation groups that may be of interest if you choose something other than a liberal arts education. If you are interested in an education focused on the Bible or on theological issues, schools accredited by the following two organizations may be of interest:

American Association of Bible Colleges
Randall E. Bell, executive director
Box 1523
130-F North College Street
Fayetteville, AR 72701
501-521-8164

Association of Theological Schools in the United States and Canada
James L. Waits, executive director
10 Summit Park Drive
Pittsburgh, PA 15275-1103
412-788-6505

Keep in mind that, while both of these accrediting groups are recognized by the Commission on Recognition of Postsecondary Accreditation (CORPA), if the Bible school you want to attend is accredited by one of these special groups—but is not accredited by one of the six regional groups mentioned earlier—you may still have problems transferring credit hours to other colleges.

Professional Accreditation

The six regional accreditation groups I've been talking about evaluate institutions as a whole. You may be interested to know, however, that there are also accrediting groups for various disciplines within a university. For example, for the discipline of business, there are two national accrediting organizations: the Association of American Collegiate Schools of Business (AACSB) and the Association of Collegiate Business Schools and Programs (ACBSP). An accreditation from one of these groups indicates that a particular division of the school has met a level of quality or expectation determined by the profession.

The differences between national accreditations for certain divisions or departments and regional accreditations that apply to the entire school are very important to understand. While both types of accreditations are considered important, credits from a division that is *not* nationally accredited can still usually be transferred to another university, as long as the university itself is regionally accredited. It is good to know which disciplines on campus are strong and have national accreditation. The truth is, however, that the average student changes his or her major twice before graduation, and so it makes much more sense to evaluate the entire university you wish to attend rather than to pick a university because of a particular faculty member or discipline. As long as the university is regionally accredited, you can feel comfortable choosing any major offered by that institution.

It is sometimes tempting to find an easy way to get a degree. Remember, however, that your goal is *knowledge,* not simply a *diploma.* Don't pursue a degree from a school for which you will have to apologize. One way to improve your chances of getting a good education is to find a school that is regionally accredited. While there are many excellent schools with other types of accreditation—and even schools with no accreditation at all—you must be aware of any limitations associated with the education and degrees they offer.

10

Excuuuuuse Me!

I've Still Got Some Questions

Q: *Why should I live on campus rather than commute?*

A: Too many students make the mistake of living off campus or at home to save a few dollars. Granted, if living at home is the only way to afford college or if living on a secular campus means having to put up with a party room, you may have no choice. Just be aware that you are giving up something. It is much harder for a commuting student to stay connected with the activities on campus. Ask any upperclassman; many college events begin after 11 P.M., long after classes are over and the library is closed. It may be toilet-papering a roommate's bed (one of the fine arts), it may be an impromptu discussion about Jesus (biblical studies), or it may be a mad dash to 7-11 for chips (physical education). Regardless of how important the activity, the bond that develops from living with others, particularly on a Christian campus, will be remembered for a lifetime.

My guess is you will complain that dumpling surprise is offered too often in the cafeteria and you will likely be awakened regularly during the night by obnoxious aliens who are posing as students across the hall, but the positive, spontaneous moments with dorm mates will far outweigh any negatives of the on-campus living experience.

Q: *What is a college fair and what should I be prepared to do if I attend?*

A: Some high schools put on what is known as a college fair for their students. This is a day when colleges and universities come to your high school campus to meet with students. Usually there is a booth for each school with at least one admissions counselor on hand to answer any questions you have about the school. This is a great time to hear from a wide variety of schools in a short period of time and pick up admissions materials for those that you are most interested in attending. Generally the schools that have representatives at such a fair are local, but some of the bigger institutions do send recruiters across the country for this purpose.

It is a good idea to get, in advance, a list of schools attending the fair, and if there are no Christian colleges invited, don't hesitate to ask your counselor to invite some. It is worth attending such a fair even if you think you know where you are going to school, because often students change their mind once they are introduced to more options.

Q: *Should I participate in an "early decision" process?*

A: If you choose to participate in the early decision process of admission, you are agreeing to apply to only one school and, if admitted, you are obligated to enroll. In turn, your file will be reviewed and processed for admission ahead of the regular applicants. This system works fine if you are absolutely positive which school you want to attend. The deadline for this type of admission is usually around November 1—nearly one full year ahead of fall classes—so if you want to pursue this option, be sure to give yourself plenty of time. Many schools do not have this plan in place but can still process a file for acceptance early.

Some students get themselves into an ethical dilemma when they commit too soon and then want to change their mind before school starts. If you think you may change your mind, you should use the regular admissions process instead. You can often apply early for regular admissions with the advantage of having no obligation beyond the potential loss of a small nonrefundable application fee.

Q: *Is the campus set up to accommodate my disability?*

A: If you are a student with a disability, the good news is that college campuses are increasingly developing more and more access for the physically and mentally challenged. However, it is your responsibility to let your counselor know after you are admitted about any special needs you may have. To keep universities from discriminating against disabled students, there are many questions that cannot be asked in the application process. Further, faculty and staff are prevented by law from asking some types of questions that would allow them to meet the unique needs you have. Because of this legislation, it is your responsibility to let appropriate campus leaders know about your disability, rather than waiting for them to discern your needs on their own.

Often there are solutions to access problems you may not have thought about. For example, just because there isn't an elevator in a multistory classroom building, it doesn't mean that a wheelchair student cannot take classes there. Likely, the course can be scheduled on the first floor to accommodate the need.

It is important to note that while colleges and universities are becoming increasingly more sensitive to the needs of disabled students, schools cannot accommodate all disabilities. There are some competencies so basic to a college education that if a student cannot meet the standard or be raised to that level, it may be better to pursue another career path than to fight about it. My experience has been that most campuses bend over backward to meet any legitimate disability request when it is called to their attention.

Q: *Is it important to consider a Christian university when my major is not one of the "Christian" vocations?*

A: If you believe, as I do, that faith impacts every area of life, then it may be argued that every major can be viewed as a "Christian vocation." I believe it is possible to be called—by God—to be a professional surfer, marketing manager, or even a camel herder. Paul was a professional tent maker. Jesus was a professional carpenter. David was a shepherd by trade. God uses all professions and uses individuals trained in all professions.

While Christian schools are, indeed, a great place to receive training for "ministry" callings such as the clergy, Christian education, and missions, the majority of students attending Christian schools are actually majoring in so-called nonreligious areas like education, business, communications, sociology, psychology, computer science, premed, history, mathematics, kinesiology, or English. You may be surprised how strong these programs are on a Christian college campus.

Q: *Am I compromising the quality of my academic education if I attend a Christian university?*

A: While a small Christian university may not have as many faculty with doctorates in your particular field of study as a large secular university, my guess is that you will have more contact with these professors than you would with faculty at the large school. This accessibility of faculty is a big factor in a truly excellent education.

Something else to consider is the importance of a shared value system. I firmly believe that students do their best work in an environment that is supportive of their lifestyle and values. I know that I learned better from professors with whom I could identify and who could have been my mentors.

If you are afraid that attending a Christian university will limit your chances to pursue the career you desire, you may want to check out some of the graduates of the school you wish to attend. One of my favorite examples is a former student of mine who is now a congressman for South Dakota. Representative John Thune was a business major and basketball player at Biola University.

Recently, in his office in Washington, D.C., we discussed his Christian college education and the important and positive role it played in his life. Indeed, John met his wife at Biola, so he got an education *and* a family out of the deal!

Q: *Are there any unexpected advantages to a Christian college?*

A: There is one big advantage of going to a Christian college that I didn't anticipate. In fact, this advantage didn't make itself apparent until about ten years after I graduated. I don't know whether I would have even noticed it if I hadn't decided to pursue a master's degree and doctorate at a state institution. Do I have your interest yet? It has to do with lifetime friends.

At the time of this writing, it is nearly twenty years since my graduation from college, and I can still tell you where at least twenty or thirty of my college friends live. Further, I would feel very comfortable giving them a call when visiting their town. In contrast, even though I did some of my master's and doctoral work more recently, I can tell you where only one fellow student from these programs lives today. The difference for me was that I had a common Christian bond with my college friends. Even if I lose track of them for a short while, I can often reconnect with them through common church connections. More than any group of friends before or after college, friends from those four years form the base of my support.

If you ask graduates of a Christian university what the high points were of their college experience, most will not comment on their major or a concept they learned in class. Despite the fact that virtually all agree they got a good education, they generally talk about people—a professor, a resident director, a friend during a time of need. Don't ever underestimate the value of Christian college friends. Consider a Christian college education as a lifetime investment.

Q: *What criteria do other kids use when making the decision to go to college?*

A: A survey of second-semester college freshmen published by the American Council on Education and the University of California at Los Angeles Higher Education Research Institute (sounds pretty official, doesn't it?) revealed that the most mentioned reason for going to college is to get a better job.[1] In the survey, the only issues that men (as opposed to women) more frequently cited as reasons to attend college were to "be able to make more money" and because "there was nothing better to do." Women were more interested than men in their desire to gain a general education and in being better cultured. The chart below gives twelve reasons why students decided to go to college, in the order of frequency of the response.

Reasons Given as Very Important in Deciding to Go to College

| | Percentage Giving the Response | | |
	All Students	Men	Women
To be able to get a better job	77%	76%	77%
To learn more about things that interest me	74	71	77
To be able to make more money	72	76	70
To gain a general education and appreciation of ideas	62	56	67
To improve my reading and study skills	43	39	46
To prove to others that I could succeed	40	39	40
To make me a more cultured person	38	32	43
My parents wanted me to go	38	37	39
Wanted to get away from home	17	17	17
A mentor or role model encouraged me to go	14	14	15
I could not find a job	7	6	7
There was nothing better to do	3	4	2

Q: *How does faith factor into a college search?*

A: Ed Hollinger in the October 1996 issue of *Campus Life* magazine[2] examines five guiding principles that answer this question:

1. *Be open to God's voice.* God speaks in symbols and through changes in our attitudes. It doesn't have to be a spoken word. In

fact more than likely it won't be. "Many of us are too concerned with making the 'right' choice. We assume there's only one 'right' choice and that all other choices are 'wrong.' But that's not always the case—especially when it comes to choosing a college. In fact, God may be willing to let us choose from several good options."[3]

2. *God speaks through others.* Here the key is to listen particularly to older friends who have been or are going to college. Even parents may have something helpful to say—it's funny that often they are the last people we ask.

3. *Mistakes are okay.* Don't miss an exciting opportunity out of fear that you will make a mistake. It is hard to accept that God works through our failures, so if you chose the wrong school, swallow your pride and transfer to another one until you feel at peace about where you are.

4. *Be patient.* Have you ever tried to make a deal with God? It goes something like this. "Lord, if I get into Big University, I'll never forget that you were the one who provided. I know I don't have the GPA and I haven't filed the application yet . . . what I need here is a miracle. I'd kind of like to know by tomorrow so I can mention it as an answer to prayer in Sunday school. Amen."

5. *God wants the best for you.* It is good to know that while we cannot rush God, he is pulling for us. We get off track when we assume our own plan is best and convince ourselves it is God's plan. I sometimes hear people fall into the trap of saying "It is God's will that I go to such and such university," when in reality it is their own desire. Then when it doesn't happen, God is blamed.

Q: *Is there really any difference in the way people treat each other on a Christian versus a secular college campus?*

A: One of the first things I hear from students who have spent time on a secular campus is how different the atmosphere is at a Christian college. By way of illustration, I'd like to tell you a true story about several students on one Christian campus who decided to find out for themselves if there were differences in how people responded on a Christian versus a secular campus.[4]

These students arranged for actors to stage a series of incidents on a Christian campus and then recreate the same incidents on a secular campus. A male and a female actor, recruited from the secular campus, posed in four different types of mishap on each campus, while the researchers observed those passing by to see if anyone was willing to help someone in need. Although the sample size was not large enough to be statistically valid, the results indicate there may be some differences in the two groups. Here is what they found:

Christian Versus Secular Campus and Differences in Willingness to Help Others

	Number of People Who Observed Incident		Percent of People Who Assisted Actor		Percent of People Who Did Not Assist	
	Christian Campus	Secular Campus	Christian Campus	Secular Campus	Christian Campus	Secular Campus
Incident 1 — A male or female actor on crutches had trouble entering and exiting the main doorway of a building and dropped books while trying to open the door.	8	17	100%	18%	0%	82%
Incident 2 — A male or female actor attempted to enter and exit a doorway while in a wheelchair.	3	5	100%	20%	0%	80%
Incident 3 — A male or female actor on crutches dropped books and papers as he or she was walking.	10	20	100%	5%	0%	95%
Incident 4 — A male or female actor on crutches dropped books and papers while walking down stairs.	3	15	100%	7%	0%	93%

Although it is doubtful that there would be this dramatic a difference between all Christian and secular student populations, the students on this particular Christian campus clearly appeared much more sensitive to the needs of others around them than their secular counterparts.

11

The First Six Weeks of College

How to Survive and Even Thrive

My guess is that you have memorized the Twenty-third Psalm. Well, here is a new psalm that I picked up through an e-mail recently. No disrespect intended.

The Student's Psalm

The Lord is my shepherd, I shall not flunk;
He keepeth me from lying down when I should be studying.
He leadeth me beside the water cooler for a study break;
He restores my faith in study guides.
He leads me to better study habits
For my grades' sake.
Yea, tho' I walk through the valley of borderline grades,
I will not have a nervous breakdown;
For Thou art with me;
My prayers and my friends, they comfort me.

Thou givest me the answers in moments of blankness;
Thou anointest my head with understanding,
My test paper runneth over with questions I recognize.
Surely passing grades and flying colors shall follow me
All the days of examinations;
And I shall not have to dwell in the university
Forever!

author unknown

Welcome to college! The bad news is that the first six weeks of school and those first exams can be pretty intimidating. The good news is that the habits you create in the beginning and the environment you create for yourself have a lot to do with how much success you will enjoy! As with most endeavors, with a little planning and preparation ahead of time, your odds of success are greatly improved.

Let's look ahead for a moment and anticipate a few of the challenges that may await you as a college freshman. By knowing what to expect—and how to prepare—half the battle is already won!

Ten Tips
for a College Freshman

1. Always wear your cleanest dirty shirt.
2. Wendy's has the best free plasticware.
3. Buy pre-highlighted books.
4. Ramen Noodles rule!
5. The secretaries run the university.
6. Dining hall food: excellent post-modern art materials.
7. Avoid spring-break trips to North Dakota.
8. Watch out for that really big building called "the cafeteria."
9. Don't be intimidated by professor's random arm movements.
10. When looking for an easy class, follow the athletes!

Adapted from "Top 140 Tips for College Freshmen" on Internet

Derailed by Distractions

For a majority of freshmen, first-year grades are some of their worst because they are too busy playing to study or they have a difficult time adapting to their new freedoms. One second-semester freshman writes:

> The thought of being told to do something or of being regimented was a put-off to me in high school because it was a kind of "need thing." When I first arrived at college, I decided to turn over a new leaf. I got new notebooks, put my schedule on the wall, and decided I was really going to be in charge. That lasted about half a week until my old self took over. What I didn't realize was how many distractions there were—mostly procrastination. There's always something more fun to do than getting to work and studying. I'll bet almost everyone faces this during the first weeks, and some never recover. I'm doing better now, partly because I don't want to fall behind again like last semester.[1]

Prepare to defend yourself from . . . the Distractors. They come in the shape of a pick-up basketball game, a roommate "making" you go out on a donut run, movie night, card games, long talks, parties, work, computer games, attempted romance, romance begun, romance disaster, romance recovery (did I mention romance?). Whatever your distraction, you will find it on a college campus. Without some accountability to a trusted friend or mentor, it may be almost impossible to stay focused when away at college.

To Sleep or Not to Sleep . . . That Is the Question

Sleep—another new-student challenge. Most freshmen don't believe in it—at least not until after 2 A.M. Between the hours of 11 P.M. and 2 A.M. the men may have a game of Frisbee football going on in the hallway, and the women can often be found discussing the campus "hunks." What can you do about it? Don't worry; I'm not going to instruct you to aim for eight hours of sleep a night, mainly because I'm not writing science fiction here. But I do have two thoughts on the matter: First, take your "body clock" into consideration as you make your class schedule. If you have only *heard* there are sunrises every morning and have yet to actually *see* one with your own eyes, don't sign up for an 8 A.M. class. If you do, you will find yourself half-dressed, running across campus, trying to catch the last half of your test. Trust me . . . I know.

Second, your mom won't be around to tell you when you need more sleep, so you may want to occasionally take a hint or two from someone else: yourself! Learn to pay attention to signals from your own body. What are some signs that you may need a good night's sleep? How about frequent colds? Or too many mornings when your head feels like a gigantic cotton ball? Or the fact that the student three doors down the hall is the one to finally march in and turn off the alarm you're sleeping through?

Eight Things NOT to Say to Your Roommate

1. I ran out of clean underwear so I borrowed yours.
2. My new drum set just arrived and my heavy metal group will be practicing in the room. Hope you don't mind.
3. I got a bad case of the munchies so I ate all your chips, hot sauce, and your sack lunch for tomorrow.
4. Sometimes my snakes get out of their cage but they usually show up in bed when they get hungry during the night.
5. I was using your toothbrush and noticed the bristles are getting a little soft. Maybe it's time for you to get a new one for us.
6. This cafeteria food really gives me gas.
7. Could I borrow your boyfriend/girlfriend? I need a date this weekend.
8. Just because your head is shaped like a lightbulb doesn't mean you're bright!

Roommate Etiquette

Roommate etiquette can be a tricky thing, especially if you have never lived in the same room with anyone before. Every year there are students who part ways because they just cannot stand each other. It is important that you enter into your relationship with a true respect for your roommate, knowing you will not survive without compromise.

Some universities have residence life questionnaires that are used to match up people with similar interests as roommates. Regardless of how you and your roommate got together, once you find yourselves sharing the same small cubicle day and night, it's time to emphasize the things you have in common and work at

Stupid Roommate Tricks

- Put your glasses on before you go to bed. Take them off as soon as you wake up. If your roommate asks, explain that they are Magic Dream Glasses. Then complain that you've been having terrible nightmares.
- Buy a telescope. Sit on your bed and look across the room at your roommate through the telescope. When you're not using the telescope, act like your roommate is too far away for you to see.
- While your roommate is out, glue your shoes to the ceiling. When your roommate walks in, sit on the floor, hold your head and moan. "Whoa! My physics prof was right! It can't be done!"
- Scatter stuffed animals around the room. Put party hats on them. Play loud music. When your roommate walks in, turn off the music, take off the party hats, put away the stuffed animals, and say, "Well, it was fun while it lasted."
- Create an army of animal crackers. Put them through basic training. Set up little checkpoints around the room. Tell your roommate that the camel spotted him in a restricted area and said not to do it again. Ask your roommate to apologize to the camel.[2]

developing a supportive relationship. Remember, your roommate has a key to the door of your room and is the only thing between you and all the pranks waiting to be played on you by the rest of your floor. Treat your roommate like royalty!

Praying for Your Roommate

On a serious note, have you ever thought about praying for the person you will live with while in college? Think about it for a moment. This is likely the first nonfamily member with whom you have roomed and a very important decision. It may be nice to dream of getting away from the monsters (also known as brothers and sisters), but you need to pray about the roommate(s) who will replace them. I was very moved to find out that my wife's parents had prayed with her when she was only a child about the type of man she would marry. Likewise, prayer that God will prepare a Christian college roommate who will understand your uniqueness and become a spiritual support may make all the difference when you get to college. Pray too that God will prepare you to be the type of roommate someone else needs.

International Roommates: Cultural Opportunity or Nightmare?

My roommate is an international student from Japan and is learning English. At the beginning of the semester, I felt just as much like an international student as she did. This is because I'm a missionary kid and have spent seventeen years in East Africa. Mia, my roommate, would often ask me questions about what certain slang words meant and often I didn't know. It was exciting to learn together with her things about the American culture that neither one of us understood. It formed a tight bond between us. She's awesome!

Keri Sivage, college freshman

131

Hirohita Nakumura arrived at the airport after a long flight to the United States from Japan. He grew up in a very traditional home, surrounded by rice paddies, on the island of Kyushu. As an exchange student from Saga University, he was very excited about attending a Christian university as he had never experienced Christian teaching at school, despite the fact that he had been a Christian for several years. On the ride to the college from the airport he was silent, watching an enormous freeway system that seemed to never end.

Finally the car pulled up in front of a four-story brick residence hall, which was very different from his home made of rice paper walls back in Japan. John Davis, his new American roommate, hopped out of the car and began to show Hirohita to their room. When John pointed to the bed, Hirohita was fearful that he would fall off in his sleep. He had always slept on the tatami mat on the floor at home. When John helped Hirohita drag the mattress onto the floor, Hirohita bowed with gratitude and approval.

As other students moved into their rooms, they had a lot to talk about. Some had attended high school together and already knew each other. No one seemed to notice Hirohita until they saw his head protruding out over the top of one of the bathroom stalls. Thinking he was pulling some prank, they opened the stall door only to find Hirohita standing on the toilet seat. Hearing the laughter and seeing the smiles on the American students' faces, Hirohita was too embarrassed to explain that in Japan they stood over a porcelain hole in the floor when using the bathroom. He had no idea how to use the Western toilets.

When John heard what had happened, he explained to the floor residents that Hirohita was from Japan and that they had unknowingly caused him to lose face during this incident. This freshman floor suddenly realized what an opportunity they had to help Hirohita and to learn a new culture at the same time. Several students invited him to join them for dinner and began involving him in student activities. In fact, Hirohita became the star of the floor intramural soccer team.

Because Hirohita had a terrible time adjusting to the food in the cafeteria and lost some weight, John and his friends often took him to a Japanese restaurant close by, and everyone was on the lookout for certain foods they knew Hirohita liked.

What happened to these students was something special. The sad fact is that many American students miss a great opportunity to room with an international student and learn about other cultures in the process because they are uncomfortable with the unknown. Often international students request American roommates, but there are not always enough interested American students to go around.

A Dozen Things to Do with an International Student or Roommate

1. Have an international night, sampling the cuisine of the international student's country and experiencing his or her culture.
2. Set up a time once a week when you can learn phrases from his or her language while he or she learns yours.
3. Look for places in your part of the United States where the international student's culture is well represented (e.g., Chinatown in San Francisco) and plan a trip there, with the international student as your host.
4. Offer to take the student home with you for a holiday like Thanksgiving, Christmas, or Easter.
5. Invite an international student to church with you and then volunteer to attend a church in another language of his or her choosing.
6. Invite an international student out for an evening.
7. Attend a meeting or event sponsored by international students on your campus.
8. Plan a trip to visit the home of an international student during the summer or after graduation.
9. Ask an international student to teach you a game and try listening to some music from his or her country.
10. Check out a book from the library that gives some history about an international student's country and then ask him or her to expand on some of the events you read about.
11. Ask about the student's family and offer to pray for them.
12. Celebrate the student's birthday and holidays important in his or her culture.

Even if it doesn't work out to have an international roommate, you may want to make a special point of befriending an international student while you are at college. Make this one of your ministries! If you want to befriend an international student but don't know how, the ideas on page 133 will help get you started.

Planning Ahead: What to Bring to School

Every year students pull onto college campuses across the country with trucks and U-Haul trailers jam-packed with all of their worldly possessions (and some of their parents' as well). Remember, you likely will have at least one roommate and if he or she pulls up with a U-Haul as well, you are both in trouble. Here are some ideas to streamline your packing:

- If you don't have to travel across the country to school, leave your winter clothes at home and pick them up when you return for Thanksgiving.
- Plan ahead by talking with your roommate(s) and deciding what items you can share and who will bring them. There's no need to have two irons and two toasters. The duplicates take up precious space.
- Be creative by using stackable crates that can be easily moved in and out of a room but take up very little space.
- Finally, many schools do not allow things like refrigerators and microwaves in the room. Call ahead or check the student handbook to determine what's allowed. Don't waste money and space bringing items you can't have.

Here is a checklist of items most students bring to college. Some of them you may not want to bother with; others your roommate may bring, so you won't have to.

Items to Share with a Roommate ───────────────────
___answering machine   ___broom/bucket
___bedspreads   ___can opener

___coffee maker

___computer/printer/surge protector

___cooking supplies

___extension cords

___furniture (bunk beds, lounge chairs, chests, etc.)

___hammock

___iron/ironing board

___lights/lamps

___microwave

___mini-refrigerator

___plastic wrap/food containers

___stereo/speakers

___VCR/TV

___waste basket

Personal Items to Pack

FAMILY/SCHOOL MEMORIES

___family videos

___high school yearbook

___pictures of friends and family

SLEEPING, BEDDING, LINENS

___blankets

___ear plugs or fan to drown out noisy neighbors

___mattress pad

___pillows

___sheets and pillow cases

___towels

___washable comforter

WASHING AND CLEANING SUPPLIES

___dirty clothes bag

___disinfectant

___fabric softener

___hand soap/soap dish

___laundry and dishwashing detergent

___paper towels

___shampoo/conditioner

___shower shoes

___toothbrush/toothpaste

FOOD AND SUPPLIES

___hot chocolate mix/coffee

___instant soup/noodles/oatmeal

___paper plates/bowls

___peanut butter

___popcorn

___sharp knife/fork/spoon

___trail mix/nuts/snack food

SPORTS/ENJOYMENT

___athletic bag/sports clothes

___backpack/gear

___baseball glove/ball

___basketball/soccer ball

___bicycle/pump/tools/water bottle

___games

___roller blades

___skis/poles/boots (not needed in Florida)

___surfboard (not needed in Minnesota)

___tennis/racquetball equipment

___video games/software

___Walkman

DESK SUPPLIES

___birthday cards
___book ends/notebooks/paper
___calendar/daily planner
___hole punch
___packing tape
___pens/pencils/sharpener/markers
___rubber bands/paper clips
___scissors
___stamps/stationery/envelopes
___tape/glue/stapler/staples

MISCELLANEOUS

___alarm clock
___Bible
___camera/film/batteries
___CDs/cassettes
___clothes hangers
___favorite books (like this one)
___flashlight
___phone card
___posters/pictures
___sewing repair kit
___sleeping bag
___smoke detector
___sunglasses

Moving In

When you pull up to your residence hall, expect the worst so you are not frustrated. Most schools have very limited time periods for students to move into and out of their rooms. As a result, everyone is there at the same time, and you will probably be unable to park close to the dorm entrance. It's a good idea to take along a two-wheel cart for moving boxes and other heavy items.

There may be a lot of confusion about your room assignment. Sometimes the residence halls are overcrowded and, as a result, three students are assigned to a room designed for two. This can be very disheartening because it may mean the room is crowded and you can't fit in all the things you brought. Keep in mind that this is usually a temporary condition and will be resolved in a matter of hours or days.

The overcrowding occurs because each year there are students who reserve a room but, for some reason, do not come to school. Your college plans on a certain number of these no-shows each semester. To keep your room charges to a minimum, the college must keep every room full and the only way to do this is to have more students scheduled for each residence hall than there are beds—with the understanding that there will be some students who never come. The challenge is to determine which students are just moving in a few days late and which students are not coming at all. Once the deadline date has passed, students are then shuffled into the open spaces and much of the overcrowding is eliminated.

Nothing can be more frustrating than to arrive on campus and find that you are assigned temporarily to a room. It may not happen to you but be prepared just in case. One way to avoid this frustration is to make your room deposit early. It's usually the students who are the last to sign up who are shuffled around.

Class Load and Time Schedule

It is often very difficult for new students to adjust to the first semester of college. Before students get to college, they often think that because they will be in class for only twelve to sixteen hours a week, college is going to be a breeze. After having five or six hours of class a day in high school, what could be so tough about having only about three hours a day in college? The difference is . . . homework. I wish I could give you a magic formula for this one, but I haven't found one yet.

In addition to daily homework assignments, there is another small problem. You will no doubt discover that college teachers have the annoying habit of assigning a bunch of projects with far-off due dates. Often you have until the end of the semester to complete the project. Now, being a good freshman, you look at the due date, say to yourself, *No problem!* then promptly classify those projects under *mañana* and go cruising. Then, before you know it, one day you are minding your own business in class when the teacher announces out of thin air, "Don't forget we have a final on Thursday and your twenty-page research paper is due on Friday." What final? What research paper? This is a joke, right? Wrong!

By the end of the day you realize that you have final exams and papers coming due in all your classes. You get out your fresh-

137

man orientation map to find out where the library is and then start looking through all the papers under your bed to see if you can figure out what you are supposed to be researching. The under-the-bed search (not to be confused with a library search) is a positive thing because you always find things under your bed that you've been looking for all semester, like a favorite mug, your swim suit, some donut coupons, and if you are really lucky, some notes from a day in class when you got serious about studying. At this point you just don't know which class the notes are from.

Next you move to a study marathon, trying to catch up. The famous "all nighters" begin as you try to read three books and two journal articles on the Civil War, write a creative story, and type a twenty-page paper all in one day. Somehow all the Cokes and NoDoz in the world can't keep you awake, and you find yourself mumbling the names of famous Civil War battles over and over in your sleep. The only problem is the reference librarian doesn't like you sleeping under the table in the Mary T. Long Memorial Reading Room, and she asks you to snore outside.

In college a good strategy is to put as much effort into developing effective study skills as you do memorizing facts and figures, at least during your first year when you are learning good study habits. Each year a large number of students flunk out of college because they misunderstood the importance of studying. You should be aware that many professors assume two hours of study outside of class for every hour of classroom time. While I don't think most students actually spend this much time in class preparation, I would think that a minimum would be to spend at least one hour of study time for every hour in class. And remember, I warned you.

Choosing Your Major

As a new student the first thing you will likely be asked is your name and the second is your major. You'll feel some pressure to have an answer when people ask you this. When I was a freshman, I decided to major in math because it was easy to spell and

I wanted a major that wasn't dominated by women. I guess I wanted to be macho. I decided on math early on so I would have an answer to everyone's second question. If the truth were known, though, I was actually unsure as to what I wanted to study. I later changed my major to business. It may have made sense to have chosen a major like nursing that is dominated by women—if my male ego could have stood it and if I had thought I would enjoy the profession. Why? Because admissions programs are looking for diversity and so are employers. When a person enrolls in a program in which he or she is a minority, that person has more chances for scholarships and, after graduation, a good job.

Take the computer field for example. Today women make up 44 percent of the overall workforce, but only 10 to 30 percent of computer programmers and engineers are women. "The number of computer science degrees awarded in the USA peaked in 1986 and by now has dropped more than 40 percent. The falloff is particularly steep for women: Currently, there are fewer than half as many women getting college degrees in computer science as there were in 1984."[3]

Yet even though fewer people—and even fewer women—are pursuing these degrees, the job market in this field is showing more promise than ever: "Through 2005, the number of computer engineers and systems analysts is expected to grow more than 90 percent, an increase of 621,576 jobs. Other tech jobs are growing nearly as quickly. College graduates in computer engineering are getting four or more job offers, often starting at $40,000 to $50,000 a year."[4]

The high-tech field has great potential for everyone, and women in the field may find themselves in even greater demand than men. It is never too early to think about how you will use your degree after you graduate and—given the amount of money you will be paying to attend college—it helps if you can avoid mistakes that would add years onto your college experience.

Remember, you don't have to choose a major before you arrive at college. You may need the first year for exploration and gaining experience. Most majors can be completed easily within your college experience, even if you do not take any classes in your major during the freshman year. In fact many schools actually prefer that you take general education classes during your first year, even if you have selected a major.

The first six weeks of your college career are characterized by decisions to be made, the excitement of being in a new place, and the mistakes that are inevitable anytime we are experiencing something for the first time. No matter how many pages you read or discussions you have with others about college, there will still be some things that no one told you about. The most important thing to remember is your relationship with Jesus Christ. My guess is that you will find it easy to remember him when things go wrong, but don't forget him when things are new and exciting. Establish a pattern of worship at school and at church as soon as possible.

12

The Parent of a New College Student

Making the Most of Your New Role

A Letter from a Mom to Her Daughter in College

Dear Child,

I am writing this slow to you because I know that you can't read fast. We don't live where we did when you left home for college. Your dad read in the paper that most accidents happen within 20 miles of home, so we moved. I won't be able to send you the address, as the last family that lived here took the house numbers when they left so that they wouldn't have to change their address. This place is real nice. It even has a washing machine. I'm not sure it works too well though. Last week I put a load in, pulled the chain, and haven't seen it since.

The weather isn't too bad here; it only rained twice last week. The first time, it rained for three days, and the second time, for four days.

The coat you wanted me to send to you, your Uncle Steve said it would be a little too heavy to send in the mail with the buttons on, so we cut them off and put them in the pockets. We got another bill from the funeral home. They said if we don't make the last payment on Grandma's grave, up she comes. John locked the keys in the car yesterday. We were worried because it took him two hours to get me and Shelby out. Your sister had a baby this morning, but I haven't found out what it is yet, so I don't know if you are an aunt or an uncle. If the baby is a girl, your sister is going to name it after me; she is going to call it mom.

Three of your friends went off a bridge in a pickup truck. Ralph was driving. He rolled down the window and swam to safety. Your two friends were in the back. They drowned because they couldn't get the tailgate down. When I found out what happened, I was glad you were away at college.

I hope all is OK at school. Not much has happened here.

Love, Mom

P.S. I was going to send you the money you requested, but the envelope was already sealed.

You brought them into the world, stayed up with them when they got the flu, and bought them their first bicycle. There is probably nothing in which you have invested more time, energy, and money than your children. Now it's time to spend the most money of all—it's time for a college education. Naturally, you are going to have strong opinions about where your child should go to school and what he or she should study. You are only interested in your child's well-being and, after all, you know your son or daughter better than anyone else. There's only one problem: Your child may not want your advice.

Sometimes this college experience can be stressful for the whole family. Striking a balance between being there for your son or daughter when you are needed and knowing when to stay out of the way when you are not is no picnic. Read carefully the contrast in comments from two college freshmen in the same class as they describe the relationship they have with their parents.

Rachel writes:

Yes, I may be old enough to attend college, but that does not mean I am mature enough or prepared enough to handle all of my adult life on my own. I still need help and guidance, even for daily life.

In contrast, Lori writes:

I know I need my education, but let me learn how to grow up on my own without you calling me five times a day to check on me. I will always love you and you'll always be my parents, but let me live and learn.

While Rachel feels a need for more guidance from her parents, Lori is feeling smothered by hers. So how do you know when to help?

Look for signals. You know it's time to help when your child unexpectedly calls to talk about something that isn't all that important, or when you find out that she or he has just encountered a disappointment. Don't interrogate, but instead look for opportunities to show your love. One of the most meaningful experiences I had with my father while in college was a note of encouragement he wrote to me on a piece of scratch paper the day I lost a race in a cross-country meet. The fact I lost the race wasn't particularly unique because I lost most of my races, but the letter was. He told me he was proud of me that day despite the fact that I didn't run as well as I would have liked. What he noticed was the fact that I had pulled the team together to pray before we ran, which he said meant more to him than my winning the race.

The fact that my father showed up to watch me run without any reminder—combined with the fact that he took the time to write me a note of encouragement—is a lifetime memory. Take the time to create a lifetime memory with your child. Here are some ideas that may help you relate better with your college-age son or daughter.

- Make an appointment to take your son or daughter to dinner. This is not the time for a trip to McDonald's. Take your child to a special restaurant. This will emphasize how special he or she is to you.
- Women love to receive flowers, especially from Dad, for no reason except that you love them.
- Attend an activity in which your child has a part: a drama, chapel service, speech, or sports event. This is probably not the time to yell out "That's my girl!" or give your son a smothering kiss. Just let him or her know you are there. Your child will appreciate the fact you came even if he or she doesn't acknowledge you at the time.
- Send an occasional care package. Favorite brownies, candy, and other treats are great to get as a surprise in the campus mail, even if your student lives at home.
- Think through in advance how you are going to react to bad grades or meeting a less-than-favorable boyfriend or girlfriend. This can be either a growing experience for everyone or a major blowup. It's your choice.
- Help your child finance a mission-type experience while in college. This is worth far more than a car or computer in molding their lives. At the same time, don't force them to go on such a trip or they may miss the point.
- Encourage your son or daughter to call home by making it easy for them (and inexpensive): Phone companies are now offer-

ing residential 800 numbers, which can be an easy way for your student to stay in touch. Or you may want to buy your son or daughter a prepaid long-distance phone card. Calling home may be less daunting if it doesn't mean a dent in the pocketbook. And make the experience on the phone a pleasant one; make sure you spend more time listening than talking.

The list below—created from interviews with second-semester freshmen—gives real-life examples of things students wish their parents would listen to regarding their college experience.

* You can't study twenty-four hours a day, seven days a week, like they want you to. You need a little fun, and it's just not the same without it.—Drew
* It actually does get very stressful.—Jamie
* Apartments are actually cheaper than the dorm.—Matthew
* The food really is bad.—Meredith
* My goal is not just being prepared for a career, but more important, being equipped as a Christian to enter into the "real world" and make a difference.—Tanya
* Their jobs may be rough, but they should try going back to school!—Seth
* I don't have to go home every weekend.—Ranell
* Don't smother me when I come home.—Cherlyn
* I really don't have time to study.—Kallie
* I am doing a lot better than I thought I would be doing, and please, please help me pay for college. I'm running out of money!—Karri
* There is more history to learn now than when they were in school.—Jon
* College, not their house, is my home now.—Kara
* You can't study before 11 P.M.—Tim

The Application Process and Campus Interview

Virginia Carey, dean of undergraduate admissions at William and Mary College, tells the story of an application she received that had an unexpected last paragraph. Despite the fact that the student's essay was good, to her astonishment the last few lines contained an emotional appeal "begging the school not to admit her." It turns out that the student had no interest in William and Mary but could not convince her parents that she preferred other schools.[1] This presented an interesting dilemma to the university because in all other respects the student met the university qualifications.

Too often well-meaning parents dominate the application process, even to the point of writing the essay or attaching notes to explain a student's need. No matter how great the temptation, remember that this is your son's or daughter's education and he or she needs to be the one to apply. Overinvolvement by parents can actually reduce a student's chances when the ethical issue of who actually wrote the essay or who is actually filling out the materials is involved. Remember, admissions counselors read hundreds of applications and have a good sense of the interests and writing style of a high school student. A discourse on family values or "why I want to go to college" from the perspective of a parent will raise questions.

Many admissions counselors say that when parents come with their child for a campus interview, the parents tend to dominate the conversation and the student rarely comments. This makes it very hard for the counselor to relate to the student. If you go to the interview, let your son or daughter do the talking and save your comments for some wrap-up questions.

Parents' Right to Know

Access to student records is determined by the Family Educational Rights and Privacy Act of 1974 (FERPA). This federal law is designed to protect the privacy of a student's education records and applies to any institution that receives funds from any program administered by the U.S. Secretary of Education. While this law applies to the vast majority of religious colleges and universities, there are a few religious institutions that do not receive or accept any kind of governmental aid and as a result are exempted.

If your child is no longer considered your dependent for tax purposes, the law means that the student is the only person who has access to his or her own education records. You will be able to get access to the records only with the student's approval. This means that you will not be able to find out your son's or daughter's grades without his or her consent. I understand why this can be difficult for parents to understand—particularly parents who are paying the tuition bill!—but please understand that this is federal law and is not up to the college or university to decide.

The purpose of this law is to protect students from having their grades and personal records made public, and it does give parents of dependent children the right to inspect and review all education records. If, for example, you believe your student's admission file is inaccurate or misleading, you do have the right to review it and ask that verifiable mistakes be corrected. Errors in such a file could influence a decision concerning admission to a college. It is important to keep in mind, however, that there are a few records that are exempted, to which you cannot have access. For example, if the school has a recommendation letter in your student's file for which your student has waived his or her right of review, this is not an accessible document. Other documents that you cannot access are:

1. law enforcement unit records
2. employment records
3. health records
4. alumni records

Colleges and universities have the right to disclose, without consent, information such as a student's name, telephone number, address, and honors if the student has not explicitly requested that the school withhold this information.[2] If your home telephone number is unlisted, you may wish to notify the school of your interest in keeping this information private or you may find it in a university telephone directory.

A Time for Prayer

While this is not always the case, it is possible for the experience of finding the right school and going though the admissions process to create tension between parents and their child. This can happen when family members are looking for different things in a college. While parents are trying to make practical decisions about instruction quality and tuition affordability, for example, students may be more concerned about finding a place where they feel they can "fit in." Angela Travers, a freshman at Regis College, describes just such a difference in priorities when she talks about a campus visit she made with her parents: "I'm standing in the dorm room looking at these people and wondering if I could live with them, and my parents are outside talking about the dirty hallway."[3] During the process of getting your son or daughter settled happily into a school, don't expect to be in sync on all aspects of the experience. Recognize that you may very well have differing goals, perspectives, and priorities.

Before these differences turn into conflicts, give God a chance to work some of them out. Express to your child your fears and concerns regarding college and let him or her do the same. Too often parents get the wrong idea that their child's acceptance to college is somehow tied to how well they have done their job as parents. There also may be an ego issue at play if you find yourself asserting that your child is good enough to get into this or that prestigious college and feeling that your reputation is on the line if he or she isn't accepted. Pray that God will deal with you and release you from negative feelings and fears. Then you can be more helpful to your child. There will likely be some things on which you will have to insist, but make sure they have nothing to do with your own ego or ambitions.

Household Changes

Don't be surprised if, after all the excitement of preparing for college, all the anticipation, and all the money spent, your freshman melts into tears when it's actually time to move away from home. Chances are you will shed a few tears of your own! It may help to know that this is a common phenomenon. Then there are other students who take off to college and never look back, and their parents, if they are honest, admit that they are ready to reclaim their home for themselves and enjoy some peace and quiet. That's okay too.

Either way, be prepared for a time of adjustment when children who have been underfoot for seventeen or eighteen years leave your home for a world of their own.

Dear Mom and Dad,

I love you as much as I always have, if not more. Just because I don't call every day or ask permission to go to the mall doesn't mean I don't care about you or don't want you involved in my life. The time has come for me to grow up, and I'm grateful for the preparation you gave me. The truth is that I can't be your little girl forever, but I look forward to growing up and sharing my adult life with you as an adult myself.

Julie Blair, college freshman

Parents expect things at home to change when the youngest child leaves, but they are often unprepared for the dynamics that accompany the leave-taking of the first or second child. For example, now that older sister is gone to college, who will sleep in her room? Who will the second child fight with? How will the chores change? Who drives which car? The list goes on and on. Don't get so caught up in getting one child ready for school that you forget how all this affects the rest of your family. Remember to make this a special time for those who stay behind.

Homesickness: A Student Disease

A common symptom of homesickness is a phone call in the middle of the night with your son or daughter crying on the other end. Further indications may be an inordinate number of absences from class or even loss of appetite. This disease is most likely to strike students who have moved away from home for the first time. If not treated, it can possibly result in the unexpected homecoming of a child who has given up on the dream of achieving a college education.

Regardless of what emotions your child's homesickness arouse in you, there are some issues that you may wish to prepare for in advance so that when the time comes, your emotions do not rule your actions. The conventional wisdom in most families is to ask the student to stick it out for at least one semester and possibly the first year. Often it takes this long for adolescents to make the adjustment to being on their own and to make strong friendships with other students. Think of college as a time of transition in a student's life. He or she has left your daily care and is beginning to make more of his or her own decisions. This maturing process takes time, and if you let your child return home prematurely, the process may be arrested, to the detriment of your child.

One exception to this is when a student is upset because he or she has encountered a hostile or compromising environment at college. While this may still prove to be a growing experience, if your son or daughter is upset about core issues, such as a roommate letting dates spend the night or a group of faculty that is antagonistic toward a Christian lifestyle, it may necessitate a change. In some instances, school authorities may be willing to step in and correct the situation once they are made aware of the problem. In others, school authorities may consider the problem simply a part of the college experience and expect your child to adjust. If the latter is true, your son or daughter may need to find a college that provides a better moral fit. Encourage your child not to give up and drop out of school entirely.

The following list gives several suggestions for helping your child cope with homesickness:

- Plan to make a trip to visit your child for homecoming weekend. This is a good time for family visits and there are often numerous activities you can enjoy with your son or daughter. (It is not necessary to be an alumnus or alumna to attend.) The timing is often good because homecoming usually takes place about six weeks into the fall semester. If your child's school has a parent weekend, this is also a good time to visit the campus.

- When you know your child is having a particularly tough day, call him or her and spend some quality time on the phone. Get used to praying together, just as you would at home in the living room, about your child's fears and loneliness.

- Send pictures or a family video regularly with updates on what is happening at home. Help your child understand that he or she hasn't been forgotten. Be upbeat on the phone and don't spend all your time explaining how much you miss your child.

- Call your child's roommates and encourage them to help you surprise your student with a special day out at your expense. It doesn't have to take a lot of money for a good surprise.

- Every few days, send a letter or postcard featuring an encouraging Scripture verse.

- If phone calls become too expensive, meet on the Internet. If you have a home computer with a modem, for as little as about fifteen dollars a month you can get unlimited access to the Internet. Most campuses now provide students with free access either through a school computer lab or hookups in dorm rooms for personal computers. You can exchange messages through e-mail or even plan a regular time for a private chat room online. I find students are much more likely to communicate by e-mail than to write and mail a traditional letter by "snail mail" (U.S. Postal Service).

Dear Mom and Dad,

The best thing about living on campus is that you meet a lot of new people and make many friends. I don't think I would have made as many friends living off campus. It is also very convenient. You can leave five minutes before class and still make it to class on time. It is also helpful, like if you need help on homework or notes, you can always find someone that is in your class who can help you. This also gives you the chance to grow up a little and live on your own, but not totally on your own!

Brandy Hamilton, freshman

Emerging Adults

College for most students is much more than just another educational step. For most it represents a transition time when they begin to emerge from under their parents' wings. There will be times you will be tempted to march over to that college and deliver a good stiff lecture to your son or daughter, or corner members of the faculty and staff and remind them that they are responsible for the well-being of your "baby" and to take good care of your pride and joy.

When these urges strike, remember that your child is on the verge of adulthood, and the last thing he or she may want is for Mom and Dad to get involved at this level. On the other hand, just when you think your child is out on his own, he will show up for some home-cooked food, bringing dirty laundry and a need to talk. Your child still needs you, but the rules are changing, and you both will have to explore new boundaries.

There is some guesswork involved at this point, because what is right in one instance will not work in another, and what worked with one child will not necessarily work with the next. My psychologist brother, Dr. Chris Linamen, after raising three children, told me that in some situations he had to "throw out the book" on raising children and go with what worked. You may have to throw out this book (preferably give it to someone else) and go with what works for you in this new family adventure.

13

Got a Problem?

Who Ya' Gonna Call? Ghostbusters?

Every day my office receives at least one call from someone who either was referred to the wrong office or was so mixed up that the caller finally dialed a random extension on campus out of desperation. You have been there, I'm sure: The operator tells you to call student services, who then refers you to financial aid, but they only handle special cases and apparently you are not special so they send you to the "zone." The zone is that special phone number that all colleges have—the number of no return. Suddenly you're on hold, listening to elevator music. After putting up with fourteen minutes of music, you hear that dreaded sound: three clicks followed by a dial tone.

This chapter is dedicated to pointing you to the right campus office, so that, hopefully, you can avoid the zone.

First of all, it is important to know that most schools are divided into two distinct areas. The first is administrative services that deal with issues relating to residence halls, student discipline, postal service, admissions, the registrar's office, food service, security, maintenance, and financial affairs. The second area is academic affairs that handle—you guessed it—academic stuff like faculty, advising, grading, classroom activities, laboratories, field trips, and class scheduling. It is confusing to many new students and their parents that, while the staff on the administrative side work year-round, many of the faculty are on nine-month contracts. So if you want to know specifics about curriculum or course descriptions, it is probably a good idea to get these answered before school is out for the summer.

Most schools have a president and several vice presidents, who preside over areas like financial affairs, student affairs, academic affairs, external affairs, recruiting, and development. The student affairs vice president usually has responsibility for things like security, chapel programming, residence life, and student discipline. Most of the new-student activities at the beginning of the semester are scheduled out of the student affairs office or the admissions office.

If you are having trouble with your bill or financing your education, generally the financial affairs division is the place to start. If you need to appeal a grade or to discuss a faculty matter, this should be handled in the academic affairs office. The external affairs or university relations office deals with alumni and church relations, among other things. Finally, the office of development cares for donor gifts and fund-raising.

Where to Go for Help

When you have a concern or problem, you need to know where to go to get answers. Here are some of the most common student concerns:

I want to talk to someone about my room assignment. Who do I call?
Try residence life or housing in the student affairs office. If you want specific information on such things as room dimensions and closet space and you know in which residence hall you will be staying, the resident director for your hall will likely be able to provide the most specific information.

I have a car and want to bring it to campus. Who do I call?

Information on car registration and parking availability is usually handled by security on most college campuses. Some campuses have parking restrictions and some colleges do not allow freshmen to bring cars to campus. All colleges and universities require some form of campus registration and a parking sticker. Check the college catalog for regulations regarding cars on campus.

I live out of state and want to know what to do with my personal things during the summer. Who do I call?

Often there is some form of storage available for students during the summer, but you probably will not be able to leave things in your room unless you are taking summer school. What you decide to bring to college may be affected by how much you can store on campus each summer. The residence life office will be able to answer your questions.

I'm finding the theological differences between the college denomination and my home church confusing. Who do I call?

I would start with your pastor. Ask him about key theological similarities or differences between your own church and the denomination of the school you are considering. Also, ask your college recruiter or admissions advisor for a visit with a campus chaplain or other students who hail from your denomination. These individuals may be helpful in explaining the spiritual makeup of the campus.

Most Christian denominational colleges have students representing many denominations. I would be more concerned about the spiritual atmosphere on campus than the denomination, unless there are some very profound theological differences that you cannot resolve in your mind.

I don't know what to major in. Who do I call?

Ask to talk with an advisor who counsels students with undeclared majors. The admissions office should know who these people are on campus and may have already assigned you to one. If after meeting with this person, you are not satisfied, don't hesitate to ask to be reassigned to someone else who can give you the guidance you need.

If I get injured, who do I call?

Campus security is usually the first contact to make concerning an injury on campus. Keep in mind that on some campuses—for your school medical insurance to cover you—you must contact an authorized school official before going to the hospital in all but the most serious cases. Your security officers will know the process. Some schools also have a campus infirmary with a nurse always on duty. It is not a bad idea to put both numbers beside the phone for easy access should a problem occur.

I need to buy textbooks. Who do I call?

The campus bookstore will have a list of books required for each course. Keep all receipts so that if there is a mix-up or if you decide to drop the class, you can return the books for a full refund. Remember, if you write your name in the book or underline the first chapters, it will be considered a used book and you will not get a full refund.

If you are budget conscious, you may want to check with the faculty member who teaches the class and ask for names of some of the students who took the class last semester. They may have a used book for sale. Some bookstores also sell used books at a reduced price, but you will usually get a better deal by buying directly from other students when you can.

I want to go to church but don't have transportation. Who do I call?

On a Christian campus there is usually no shortage of cars going out to church on Sunday morning. Just let your resident assistant know that you are looking for a ride. Often churches in a college town will provide van or bus service between the church and campus. Many large secular schools have campus churches within walking distance of or right on campus. A couple quick phone calls to a local church of your choosing will generally produce results as well. It is a weak excuse to skip church because you don't have a ride, but you may have to do a little advance planning to make it happen.

Eleven Excuses for Missing Class

1. I never dreamed I'd get so sick from eating twenty-five live goldfish!
2. Someone called and told me class was canceled. Gee, I guess they had the wrong number.
3. My father's brother's sister-in-law's son's best friend was rushed to the hospital. We consider him part of our extended family.
4. I got a spoon caught in my ear.
5. My alarm is the only one that didn't go off in the whole state this morning.
6. Before I tell you why I missed class, could you tell me again what qualifies as an "excused" absence?
7. Oh, I know what you are thinking, but it isn't the same as the other eight classes I missed. This time I really did over-sleep.
8. The weatherman really blew it. He said last week to expect heavy rain, so I didn't dare go out.
9. No one ever understands, so there is no point in explaining.
10. The devil made me do it.
11. Let's forget it ever happened, and next week I'll buy donuts.

I have to miss a class. Who do I call?

Regardless of the excuse, most professors appreciate the courtesy of a phone call from students who will not be in class. Obviously I'm not talking about awakening them at their home at 4:45 A.M. after you've just thrown up last night's pepperoni pizza. A better option is to leave a message on departmental phone mail or wait until office hours to phone your professor. If he or she is not available, leave a message with the department secretary.

I am interested in drama or a singing group. Who do I call?

Start by calling the fine arts department. There are often try-outs before school begins or during the first part of the school year, so don't wait very long to get this information. You may also want to ask about scholarships that may be available for students talented in acting or music.

I'm interested in writing for the campus newspaper. Who do I call?

Campus papers are usually under the auspices of student government, with a journalism professor as their campus advisor. Contact the student government office, the journalism department, or the newspaper office to find out how to get involved.

I need to drop a course. Who do I call?

Start with your advisor. If you don't have an assigned advisor, call the department of your declared major or see the undeclared advisor. You'll want to keep in mind that some classes are not offered every semester, so dropping a course may set you back in your overall plan for finishing college. Further, if you are receiving any form of financial aid, it is important to find out if dropping a class may impact your grants and loans due to the reduced number of credit hours you will then be taking. It is also important to find out whether or not you will receive any tuition refund before you make your final decision.

If all else fails, every campus has secretaries who know how to get things done. Find one of these individuals on your campus and then bribe him or her regularly, because everyone knows these people really run the college!

14

The Challenge
of Changing Schools

Insights for Transfer Students

Whatever reason you have for transferring to another college or university, you are not alone. The National Center for Educational Statistics tells us that among those students beginning their post-secondary education in 1989–90, more than one in three students (35 percent) had transferred by 1994.[1] That's a whole lot of ya'll (Texan for you guys).

So you are not crazy because you want to change schools, but you do need to get in touch with why you wish to transfer. For some of you, your job or family has moved and you have chosen to move too. Others of you have completed the two-year program at a community college and you are planning to continue school at a four-year institution. And still others are not happy where you are. In all of these cases, you are now faced with "breaking up" with your current college.

It is not at all uncommon to find yourself feeling like you want to stay at your present college one day while the next you can't wait to get out. That's because your present school has provided many positive experiences, even if it is proving not to be the right fit for you. It may help to know that many students consider transferring and walk through the entire process of applying to another institution and then decide to stay where they are. Sometimes it helps just to know what your options are.

If you are ready to look into another school, many of the previous chapters will apply to you. This chapter, however, will address some additional issues.

Transferring Credits

One of the challenges of being a transfer student is trying to learn all the ins and outs of the school. Transferring into a new school is difficult. I wasn't well informed about what I needed to do when I came. There were some things I needed to do and classes I needed to take that I wasn't told about until I was almost a junior. So now I am having to run around and make sure I have all the classes I need to graduate.

michelle m.

Your first and greatest concern is probably how the credits you have already completed will be handled by your new school. It's generally true that the further along you are in school, the more likely it is that some of your credits will not transfer. It's important to remember that even if credits transfer, it doesn't mean that they fulfill a requirement for graduation.

One reason some course credits may not transfer to another university is the differences in accreditation (see chapter 9). Another reason is the nature or content of the course. There are professors who have incorporated a unique dimension into their course, making it different from similarly named courses offered at other schools and, as a result, they do not believe you should be excused from taking their course. There are some professors who act as if God has gifted them to be one of very few earthlings who can teach the course correctly, and they never think credit should be transferred.

It is common to encounter problems if you try to transfer advanced classes from a community college into a four-year school. For example, if you are an accounting major at a community college and want to take as many classes as possible to help you toward your four-year degree, you will probably want to take everything the community college offers in accounting, right? Negative on that one! While the basic first-year courses will generally transfer, courses like advanced accounting, auditing, or cost accounting likely will not transfer to a four-year school. The general principle is that any course considered a junior- or senior-level course at a four-year school should not be taken at a two-year school. Even if you use the same textbook as is used at the four-year school, you may not be successful in getting the course transferred.

Another sticky situation can occur when students from a Christian university try to transfer a large number of Bible credits to a secular school. Generally a few courses will transfer, meeting history or other general requirements, but students with twenty-five or thirty hours of Bible may not be able to transfer all of them. Having said this, I want to remind you that part of the reason for going to a Christian university is to study the Bible. Often you can do so under some of the best Christian scholars in the country. If you are going to transfer, possibly the best thing you could do before you leave is to take some Bible courses, knowing that this is an investment in your future, whether or not you will be able to transfer the credits. Many students who do not plan to graduate from a Christian school come there exclusively for the Bible courses. Don't miss the opportunity.

Meeting Graduation Requirements

As a transfer student you must take the responsibility to check with the registrar of your new school to find out how many credits you are able to transfer, how many of the courses fulfill graduation requirements, and what requirements are outstanding that you must complete before graduation. For example, if you ask your advisor if a particular history course will transfer, the answer is often yes. However, on closer examination, you may find out that this particular history course can only be used for elective credit, which means that you will likely need to take another university-approved history course to meet the general education requirement. When I talk about "general education requirement" in this context, I'm referring to a basic block of courses or disciplines that all students must complete to graduate, regardless of their major, at a given university. In this example, if you like history and need several elective courses to graduate anyhow, another history course may be no problem. But if you thought you had already taken all of your history only to find out shortly before graduation that you will be at school another semester because you haven't taken the "right" history course, that can be pretty disheartening.

If too many of your courses transfer in as elective credits rather than required courses, you may find yourself spending several extra semesters in school taking the required courses. Make sure you have a good understanding of exactly how your credits will be evaluated at your new school before making the transfer.

An Official Credit Evaluation

There is a way to avoid the shock of learning (too late) that your new school won't apply many of your credit hours toward graduation: Ask to have an official evaluation of your credits made before you decide to transfer. I don't recommend that you ask for an official evaluation from every school you are considering, since this is a time-consuming process for the registrar. Make it a last step or possibly the deciding factor between two finalists and allow plenty of time for the school to respond.

It's possible that when you make this request, some schools will tell you they cannot provide this information until after you enroll. This is where you may need to bring along some muscle to convince them that you need the information. If you do not have a very large mafia-style friend, you may find that a persuasive mom or dad can do a pretty decent job of convincing a school counselor to help you out.

In evaluating transcripts, some universities use a "common course numbering system" or equivalency guide by which they have already decided the courses that will transfer, based on prior agreements. Make sure a counselor gives you, in writing, a list of the specific courses that will transfer and what requirements they will meet so you can avoid any misunderstandings later.

If you know that you are going to transfer, or think that there is some chance, it is best to take basic courses that most schools will accept. If you are not sure what these are, call a couple of schools that you think you might be transferring to and run the courses by

---

Signs a Transfer Student Has Been in College Too Long!

1. You think spring break is a national holiday.
2. You wonder how one of your papers got to the Dead Sea.
3. You wear your own clothes to the Retro-Seventies theme party.
4. On the first day of class at your new school, the rest of your class thinks you're the instructor.
5. Your freshman registration at the first school was on papyrus.
6. You still use your Mod Squad binder and thermos.
7. You can recall burning your Civil War draft card at another college.
8. You've worked with eight student loan officers at various schools and now they ask your advice.[2]

them in advance. You may need to fax them a copy of some course descriptions from your catalog and possibly even send the syllabus from the course. If you know where you are going to transfer, most schools have prior-approval forms that can be filled out and signed, guaranteeing that they will accept the courses you plan to transfer, provided you don't change classes. If you know where you will transfer well in advance and if you plan your schedule carefully, there is no need for you to have to lose credits when you transfer.

Appealing a Transfer-Credit Decision

Despite the fact that you may take all the appropriate precautions, you still may lose a few credits when you transfer or end up with extra electives. Before you give up on how many credits you need to retake, it may be worth appealing your case. Many students appeal transfer-credit decisions and win.

Generally, staff members in the admissions or registrar's office evaluate your credits. They are generalists by training and cannot possibly be knowledgeable about all the details of every class. As a result, they sometimes make decisions that are worth challenging. In most institutions the final decision comes from the faculty in the department where the class is taught. If you feel the evaluation is too harsh, you may wish to take a copy of your course syllabus, the course catalog description, and your textbook to a faculty member for a more careful look. Keep your coursework, books, and syllabus in case you need them later to make such a case.

Another option is the appeals process. Many schools have a formal appeals process, with detailed steps to follow in challenging a university decision. This process is generally very time-consuming, so it is not a good path to take if you need immediate results, but it may be the only option available to you. If you decide to use this process, be as concise and articulate as possible in explaining in writing why you feel the committee should decide in your favor. Remember, if they don't, you may be spending considerably more time retaking classes than it would take to make a strong case. Let someone who is not emotionally involved in your situation read your case and offer objective advice. Finally, if you are offered the opportunity to represent your case in person, do so, even if it means taking a vacation day from work. It is harder to say no to someone in person.

Don't expect to get everything that you think you are entitled to just because you feel strongly about your request. In some cases a professor or committee that knows much more about the educational process may be trying to improve your educational experience and you may be hurting yourself by asking for too much. It is generally not very helpful to allege discrimination or force the issue beyond an appeals process or a friendly visit with a professor. The point here is to exhaust all available options in a professional, Christian manner but not to turn your future university against you in the process.

CLEP Tests

If you are not successful in getting a class transferred, or if it doesn't meet the needed general education requirements, you may wish to try another approach. The College Board offers a rather extensive group of College Level Entrance Placement (CLEP) exams, which, if passed, are accepted for college credit in more than 2,800 colleges in the United States. Administered at more than 1,200 locations, these exams are completed in one ninety-minute sitting and generally cost much less than the tuition for an equivalent course in college.[3] Options for credit are available in the following subject areas:

General Examinations ——————————————————————————

English Composition	Natural Science
Humanities	Social Sciences and History
Mathematics	

Subject Examinations ——————————————————————————

Accounting	Analysis and Interpretation
American Government	of Literature
American History I	Business Law
American History II	Calculus with Elementary
American Literature	Functions

College Algebra
College Algebra-Trigonometry
College French
College German
College Spanish
Educational Psychology
English Literature
Freshman College Composition
General Biology
General Chemistry
Human Growth and Development

Information Systems and
   Computer Applications
Introductory Sociology
Macroeconomics
Marketing
Microeconomics
Principles of Management
Psychology
Trigonometry
Western Civilization I
Western Civilization II

Some students do not consider this option for receiving legitimate college credit because they are afraid they may not pass the CLEP test. Actually, the success rate is higher than most students realize. Many schools consider a C grade to be passing on these tests. Since no grade is recorded, it really doesn't matter if you do just barely pass. Further, since there is no record placed on your college transcript if you don't pass, the most you have to lose is the cost of the test and the time you spent taking it. Take a little time to review the courses that didn't transfer and then see if you can test out of them. For more information on CLEP, contact your admissions counselor or go to the source at: College Level Examination Placement, P.O. Box 6601, Princeton, NJ 08541-6601.

Remember, not all schools will accept this credit and some will only accept certain CLEP exams, so make sure to check with your next school before you take these tests.

When to Transfer

"Transferring after your first year is a really bad idea. You just can't judge a school by freshman year. Wait, and things may be a lot better as a sophomore."

(Half the people interviewed)

"If there's any advice I have, it's don't wait. Get out as soon as possible. If you hate school, there's no reason to go back for a second year. . . ."

(The other half)[4]

The jury is still out concerning when it is time to move on to another school. Some students report that transferring between the fall and spring semesters can be a real challenge because most of the friendships and room assignments have been in place for at least three months. This makes it very difficult to break into the crowd.

On the other hand, if your concern is the acceptance of your credits at the next college, mid-year may be the time to change schools because the fewer credits you have to transfer into another school, the less chance for wasted courses. One additional semester may add to the number of courses lost.

An issue to keep in mind before transferring to another school is an academic hurdle called a "residency requirement." Most schools want all their graduates to have a specified minimum of thirty to sixty credits taken in residence at their school. This means that if you are a senior and want to transfer, even if you need only twelve more credit hours to meet another school's academic requirements, you may end up needing as many as sixty more hours to meet their campus residency requirement. The reason for a residency requirement is to make sure that anyone who is granted a diploma from a given college or university has received a significant portion of their education from that university. With no residency requirement, it would be possible for a student to take all their classes at other schools and then shop for an institution somewhere in the country where they could package their courses to get a degree. While the residency requirement makes some sense, it can be a nightmare for upper-class transfer students.

Articulation Agreements

Articulation agreements are formal understandings between schools as to what they will accept from each other in the way of transfer courses. These agreements are usually course-by-course specific and are most commonly found between community and four-year colleges. Of course, it is not possible for one college to have agreements with every other college or university in the country, so these written agreements are most commonly found between schools in the same geographic region. It may be well worth your time to find out from a counselor what institutions have formal transfer agreements with your school. Ask for copies of articulation agreements from schools that might be of interest and do some of your own transfer analysis.

Transferring for Athletes

If you are currently involved in a university athletic program, it is important for you to discuss with your next school how transferring may affect your future eligibility to participate in sports. In some cases, transferring from one university to another could result in your losing one valuable year of eligibility. The NCAA and NAIA athletic associations both have detailed rules concerning transfer students. Know your options before you change schools.

The Emotions of Transferring

You may be able to find a school that meets all your needs and where the vast majority of the classes you have already completed can be applied toward your degree. What you may not be prepared for is the emotional process of separation from your existing school and the friends you have made there. The majority of students do not tell their college friends that they plan to transfer until just before they leave due to the anxiety they feel over their future separation. For most of us there is no easy way to say good-bye, so many students focus instead on what is up ahead. The sooner you can make some connection with students and faculty at your new school, the easier it will be to make this transition.

One last thought: You will always be welcomed back at a school you have decided to leave. If you transfer for the wrong reasons, or feel you made a mistake and are out of God's will, it's not the end of the world. Swallow your pride and get back on track, even if it means returning to the school you recently left.

15

Distance Learning

The Next Best Thing to Being There

Immediately following the guest speaker—a top strategist on the Civil War—the class discussion began with a flurry. Before long the whole class was involved in a heavy debate regarding some of the Civil War tactics used by Sherman in burning Atlanta. Finally the instructor, Dr. Wilson, chimed in to cool everyone down and show a video of the events leading to Sherman's sweep of the South.

Normally Todd could be accused of flirting with his classmate Carol because he always seemed to find a way to make a flattering comment on her outfit or her jewelry, but today he stayed focused on the discussion, with little clowning around. Maybe he was in a serious mood because he was actually home, sick with the flu, participating in the class discussion from his kitchen table. Or perhaps he took exception to the comments on Sherman because he was connecting to class from Pittsburgh, Pennsylvania, in the heart of Union country.

Carol, on the other hand, was taking class by live video at work in Atlanta (a Confederate stronghold), where her family had lived for the last one hundred years. The instructor was teaching from her office at a Christian college in the Midwest, and the guest speaker was lecturing from the Smithsonian, where he pointed out artifacts in the museum as he spoke. The class was made up of students from throughout the nation, sitting in front of personal computers equipped with small video cameras.

The first few weeks, students were a little distracted by the technology, but before long discussions proceeded as though everyone were in the same room. Class discussions were often lively and informal. In fact, from time to time students liked to tease Dr. Wilson about the mess in her office that they could see behind her via the video camera.

After class Todd sent an e-mail message to Carol apologizing for his strong position in class and asked her for permission to set up a direct video connection so they could communicate in private. I'm not sure whether Todd wanted to apologize again or whether he wanted to catch up on the flirting he had missed during the last class session. I will let your imagination finish the story.

Today classes are being offered by two-way video phone lines, by satellite, and over the Internet. It is possible to get a bachelor's and master's degree from accredited schools without ever stepping foot on a college campus or actually seeing the teacher in person. And while it is not likely that distance learning will ever completely replace the special atmosphere created on a college campus—after all, there is no substitute for grabbing a cup of coffee after class with a professor or meeting friends for lunch in the cafeteria—distance learning does bring the classroom experience to students who would not otherwise be able to attend college.

It is likely that some form of off-site educational opportunities will be experienced by an increasing number of students. Some will take a combination of traditional classes complemented by an assortment of video tapes, Internet sessions, correspondence segments, and online experiences, which, all combined, will add up to a college degree. If you are not in a city where you have access to the type of education you want and cannot go away to school to get it, the good news is that there are a number of schools beginning to offer classes in these formats.

Questions about Distance Learning

Can I afford the technology?
For a little more than the price of a mid-level computer, you can now access a distance education. Generally, if you can't afford a given kind of computer today, it will likely be half the price in a matter of a few years. I strongly recommend that you find the college program you wish to take before you purchase the computer equipment, so you can meet the exact specifications of the institution.

You will spend considerably more in tuition than you will on technology, so while there is some up-front expense involved, the computer should not be the barrier to your education. Some colleges and universities can even offer you an educational discount on a computer, making it substantially cheaper than what you would pay in a retail store.

How will I buy my books?
While a college bookstore is a nice convenience, you'll find that it's hardly necessary. As a long-distance student, you will pick up your syllabi on a computer bulletin board, along with a listing of books that you can order from any local bookstore. Global bookstores—such as Amazon (www.amazon.com)—are also available through which you can purchase virtually any book in print with a credit card on the Internet. In the last fiscal year Amazon sold sixteen million dollars worth of books to 180,000 customers in more than one hundred countries.[1] Apparently some people find this to be a good way to purchase their books, and there is no reason textbooks cannot be purchased this way as well.

If I take classes by distance learning, how will I do my library research?
You probably already have access to many library services via local community colleges, universities, and public libraries. Almost

every library in the country allows visitors to use some of their library resources free of charge. You may not be able to check out a book or use the interlibrary loan services, but access to computer databases, books, and reference materials are often available free on-site. Just be prepared to spend some time there to do your work (remember, librarians don't like you sleeping under the tables in the reference room).

In addition to these traditional library services, there is an increasing amount of help available on the Internet. For example, if your assignment is to do research on the evolution of flight, an Internet search would lead you to Web sites on the Wright brothers where you can study photos of their first flight, read articles written by Orville and Wilbur Wright, locate a bibliography of books written on the subject, and even find links to materials at the Library of Congress.[2] Similar materials can be found for the Red Baron,[3] Amelia Earhart (in English or Spanish),[4] and the U.S. Air Force Museum.[5] Even more obscure are references for such subjects as Korean War airplanes. One of the home pages listed was on nose art. I had never seen a web page on nose art so I checked this one out. It turned out to be Dawn Kuczwara's collection of the art soldiers painted on noses of their planes.[6] This shows the depth of resources available. It is worth noting that much of the material on the Internet is *not* academically sound. Review your research carefully before using it in an educational setting.

If you still think that you need a library, there is a virtual library available on the Internet, which for a small monthly fee can provide full text access to a variety of resources. When I researched this, not all the mainstream publications were available, but there were a substantial number of resources available for research.

How do I take tests and hand in assignments if I am not in a normal classroom?

While some teachers offer tests online, others will ask you to have your test proctored by a librarian or other designated person. The location in which you take your test may vary, but its format will probably be very similar to what you would experience in a traditional class. Other assignments may be sent to you by mail, as a computer attachment on the Internet, or by some type of courier service.

What happens when a professor wants to show a video or overhead in class?

There are several formats for distance learning. One of the most popular—the two-way interactive video format over phone lines—offers teachers an amazing array of multimedia options. By using this format, for example, an instructor can transmit, right to your computer, a video on personality disorders for your psychology course, or link you to a video camera so that you can observe a simulated chain reaction in a chemistry class. Interactive video has the capability of showing slides of a trip through Israel in a Bible class or a Powerpoint slide presentation on the structure of local government in political science. Finally, the teacher can discuss a handout he forgot to make copies of before class by using a document camera to show a standard sheet of paper on the monitor. Virtually all teaching tools that are available in the classroom can be transmitted by computer, with the exception of those that require human contact.

Where is the best place to look for a distance learning program?

I know you think I'm Internet happy, but the truth is that the Internet college home pages are the best source of distance learning options. Further, since new distance programs are emerging daily, many college catalogs do not offer up-to-date information on all these new programs. As I've mentioned before, it is always a good idea to stick with regionally accredited institutions (chapter 9) for these and other programs.

Can I get a college degree while living overseas?

Theoretically, yes. As long as you can access an Internet connection, there should be programs available to you. I can think of only two complications: First, you may need to allow extra time when turning in assignments via international mail. Also, you may need to get special permission to wear pajamas during class, since global time zone differences mean you could be participating in live chat sessions in the middle of the night.

174

What is the downside of distance learning?

I am convinced that some of the best educational experiences happen outside the classroom. Whether these experiences include the time your class visits a homeless shelter or the time you stay up till 3 A.M. discussing business ethics with your roommate, don't discount the value of human interaction in your education. Study groups are much more difficult to achieve online and the spontaneous activities of catching a game of pool with a friend or staying up all night to decorate a neighbor's room for his or her birthday are important parts of the college experience that distance learning cannot offer. The chapel and devotional opportunities that are at the very core of a Christian college experience are also very difficult, if not impossible, to capture in a distance environment. Possibly the most significant loss to the distance student is the loss of lifetime friendships that develop between faculty and students. One cannot begin to explain how much more college entails than a lecture three days a week. Don't assume that the wonders of technology can make up for all of this.

Summary

Distance education has the capability of bringing together a global audience under some of the best teachers in the world. It also has the capability of isolating us more completely from each other. Thanks to modern technology, we can shop, read, entertain ourselves, arrange for travel, make investments, talk to our relatives, and do our jobs without ever stepping out of our home or meeting anyone face-to-face. Receiving an education can now also qualify as an in-house convenience. The good news is that this opens up tremendous possibilities for students who otherwise would not be able to earn a college degree. The bad news is that distance education may create a new global order where alumni don't recognize each other and any sense of loyalty to an alma mater may be a thing of the past. While technology brings a new excitement to education, it also challenges the basic tenets of the college experience. Think carefully as you weigh advantages and disadvantages of this new mode of education.

16

Okay, So I'm an Adult
Who Wants a Degree

Educational Choices for Grown-Ups

Maybe you are reading this chapter because you have found the time or the courage to return to college after a long absence. Or perhaps you began reading this book to help a son or daughter prepare for college and found your interest piqued by the topic of this chapter. Regardless of how you got here, if the thought of going back to school has crossed your mind, it's possible that it has been accompanied by some anxiety.

Adult-Student Myths

Do any of the following myths sound familiar?

Myth 1: I'm too old to return to school.
Adult learners now make up more than 40 percent of the nation's college students. These adults range in age from twenty-

five to eighty-five years of age. One recent graduate, Dorothy Waters, began her college education in 1933 and earned seven credit hours at Iowa Wesleyan College before her education was interrupted by marriage. Sixty-four years later, at the age of eighty-one, Mrs. Waters was awarded her bachelor of arts degree in English from the University of North Texas. Fourteen great-grandchildren attended their grandmother's graduation to see her achieve a lifelong dream. And if this great-grandma has her way, in a few years they will all be back watching another graduation ceremony. Mrs. Waters plans to do graduate work.[1]

Given the dramatic change in our society, we can no longer plan to keep the same job for a lifetime, so the need for learning and continued education has become even more important, whether we are eighteen or eighty-one. Education happens to be the best prevention of finding yourself in an unemployment line. On the other hand, your choice to go back to school may have nothing to do with job security. It may stem from the need to fulfill a lifelong dream or a need to learn. Regardless of your reasons, you are never too old to go to college.

Myth 2: My memory isn't as good as it used to be, so I probably can't take tests and write papers.

A good memory is a definite asset. It is not, however, a necessity for completing your education. Most adults find that they are still very capable of learning and, if they have lost anything in the way of memory, they typically make up for it with study skills that are better than those of their younger counterparts. Here are a couple suggestions to help you cope with returning to college life and achieving the best possible grades and test results. Knowing how you will deal with various obstacles in advance should help reduce some of the anxiety about returning to school.

1. *Set up a study center.* If you can find a room or desk to claim as your own so that you don't waste valuable minutes every time you need to study, it will make you more efficient. In addition, a good study environment will improve your concentration.

2. *Plan for emergencies.* Too often adult students have to drop classes or miss critical class sessions because they haven't planned for emergencies. Make plans in advance for what you will do

when your children are ill or when your car breaks down. Allow enough time in your schedule to compensate for unplanned events and decide in advance how you will deal with as many emergencies as you can think of. Contrary to what you may think, it is possible to plan for the unplanned.

3. *Find some time for yourself.* Let's face it. There is more to life than changing diapers, mowing lawns, and cramming for tests. You will cope much better if you take some time during the week to do something you enjoy. You may plan to watch your favorite TV show, go golfing, or read something just for fun. Don't make life all work or you will burn out before you finish.

4. *Divide your assignments into manageable parts.* When you have a twenty-page research paper, you may wish to break down the work something like this:

a. Visit library to select a topic
b. Read articles on topic
c. Create writing outline
d. Conduct additional research
e. Write first half of rough draft
f. Write last half of rough draft
g. Edit draft with third party reader
h. Produce final copy

It may be motivating to put each step on a written checklist so that you can monitor your progress and see the success you have made.

5. *Delegate to others.* If you add class and study time to your schedule, you will need to learn how to assign tasks to your children. Teach them how to wash clothes, mow the lawn, or make their own school lunch to help reduce your workload. Hire outside help if necessary so that you can concentrate on your studies.

6. *Learn to say no.* All too often people take on college courses without turning down any other responsibilities. Remember, people will still be your friends and care about you even if you have to temporarily turn down that PTA assignment, Sunday school request, or racquetball game.

7. *Don't procrastinate.* It takes the same amount of time to complete an assignment three weeks ahead as it does to struggle to do the assignment the night before it is due. The difference is the amount of stress you create with the latter approach.

If you learn to follow these basic concepts, I think you will be pleasantly surprised at your success with regard to tests and assignments.

Myth 3: I'm concerned that if I don't get good grades, my employer will be dissatisfied with me.

More often than not, the fact that you have chosen to go back to school will impress your employer more than any grade you may receive in class. Most employers are thrilled to have better-educated employees. Letting your employer know how well you do in school is far less risky to your career than the absence of a degree.

Myth 4: I didn't do well the first time I was in school, so I must not be college material.

As we review student records for admission into graduate school, we look at applicants' overall grade point average and the GPA from their last sixty credit hours. Nine times out of ten, when a student has returned to college as an adult, his or her GPA is higher for those courses than it was the first time he or she was a college student. For a variety of reasons—many of them obvious—adult students often fare much better than they did when they were nineteen and fresh out of high school.

Myth 5: I'm really too busy with my job and family to go back to school.

my greatest concern about returning to school is having enough time to "do it all." I'm a mother of three, work full-time at a stressful job, and I had no study habits. High school was so easy for me and my brief encounter with college after high school was a nightmare. I was very apprehensive about finding time to study without taking time away from my family and without my job performance *suffering in any way. It's been a tough road and I'm not at the end of it yet. But my family has been supportive as have my coworkers and superiors. The experience has been a positive one in my life.*

michelle Dusbabek

Your spiritual life and family responsibilities should be your first priority. You may wish, however, to reevaluate what you are doing with the rest of your time. With the advent of classes by Internet; live, two-way interactive video accessible via your personal computer; and courses offered at corporate workplaces rather than just on the college campus, people who in the past could not attend school are now returning in record numbers.

The following time-saving tips were given by adult students:

- Eat a bag lunch on the way to class.
- Attend class. It cuts down on study hours.
- Keep your class notes in your car and review them whenever you have a minute, for example, waiting at the doctor's office or in the drive-up line at the bank.
- Schedule time to study.

Adult-Student Questions

I understand you can receive credits for life and work knowledge. Are these legitimate programs?

The concept of receiving academic credit for life and work knowledge has emerged in the past twenty years as a viable alternative to a traditional education. Many colleges and universities both large and small have found that adults have gained valuable knowledge in the workplace. Generally through an extensive process of preparing a portfolio, which contains documentation of in-service training, books read, knowledge gained through work assignments, and so on, an adult student can earn credit for a year or more of course work, saving valuable time and money.

180

The better programs involve several evaluators who read each portfolio to determine whether or not quantifiable learning has occurred. Generally adult students find that they have accumulated much more knowledge that will count toward a college degree than they ever thought possible. Often the missing element in an adult's on-the-job education is the theory behind the steps they take at work. This area can be supplemented by an individualized degree plan once the portfolio has been completed.

The good news is that some of the best programs in the country for adults are at Christian colleges and universities. Some of these programs have numerous degree possibilities while others have one lockstep track where the group takes courses together.

The legitimacy of the degree has more to do with the legitimacy of the school than the nature of the program. If your degree is in the adult program at DePaul University, for example, you carry all the credibility of that school with your degree. At Dallas Baptist University we offer this kind of portfolio class, and many of our graduates go on to pursue master's degrees and doctorates from great schools across the country. The key again is to make sure that you attend a regionally accredited institution (see chapter 9) to complete your undergraduate degree.

Some graduate programs will accept you into their program but may not accept portfolio credit for prerequisite courses, so you may need to take these classes in a traditional setting. If you know that you plan to go on to graduate school, I suggest you find out which courses a graduate school requires and not petition these courses for credit in your portfolio process. Some schools have certain tracks in their adult programs designed specifically to prepare students for graduate school.

If you meet the necessary degree completion requirements for entrance to your program of choice, such a program can save you valuable time and money.

Even if you are not quite ready to begin your program, you can start gathering materials for your portfolio, such as old certificates from training programs, letters from bosses commending you for a project you completed, and a resume or autobiography. Even if you decide not to return to school, the process of documenting your accomplishments can increase your self-worth and motivate you to do even more with your life.

Why should I go back to school?

The glass ceiling is not a myth! Even though I have eighteen years employment with my company and ten years field experience, I am still not considered on a level with even first-year graduate students with no experience. Unfortunately I don't make the rules—but I have to play by them. It was either get degreed or get the shaft. I chose the hard road—full-time employment, full-time student, full-time wife and mother.

Mary Davis

Most adult students I interviewed mentioned a desire to be better prepared for the job market. Several expressed concern about being trapped doing the same type of work for twenty to thirty years. Others were tired of working for incompetent managers and felt that a degree would give them the necessary edge to move up themselves. And finally, several were getting a degree to fulfill a childhood dream. Each of the adults interviewed for this book acknowledged the serious commitment that was necessary to complete a degree and were willing to make college a priority. None of them said it was easy, but none regretted making the decision either.

How can I tell if a program is "adult friendly"?
Just because a school offers an adult program doesn't mean it is "adult friendly." Look for clues that will help you determine how serious the institution is about meeting the needs of its adult students.

- Are there registration periods in the evening and on weekends or do you have to take time away from work to register for classes? In the best-case scenario, registration should be offered at times that are convenient to both traditional and adult students.

- Does the school have any special payment program for working students? To help adult students, some institutions have instituted a "third-party agreement" where students are excused from any up-front tuition payment. This is because many employers will pay for your tuition—but usually only at the end of the semester. Some schools, Dallas Baptist University included, will postpone billing adult students until classes are complete, with the understanding that the employer will come up with the tuition money. This can be helpful to family cash flow.

- What is the policy on food in the classroom? If the school is adult friendly, you can usually drink and eat during class, because you missed dinner while commuting between your office and the classroom. As a word of caution, however, let me say that picnicking on the floor or having pizza delivered to your classroom doesn't seem to go over well with professors (I know this because I found out the hard way), so keep it reasonable.

- Does the school have a history of being tolerant when students are unexpectedly sent away on business by their employer? While standards must be established against constant absences and tardiness, there should be some leeway given when work commitments collide with school.

- Do the instructors know how to teach adults? On every campus students complain about some of the professors. The key here is not how popular teachers are or whether anyone ever complains about them, but how they engage adult students. Is the lecture condescending, or does the instructor take advantage of the rich wealth of knowledge brought into the room by adults? On adult friendly campuses the professor's role with adults is that of a facilitator.

- Are there any adult honor societies or social groups on campus? Even though you may not have any interest in an honor society at this point in your life, organizations like this serve as good indicators of the university's commitment to adult students.

- When are classes offered? Most schools that offer adult programs hold classes in the evenings and on weekends. It is now possible to complete a whole degree on weekends at many schools. You may also want to look for different class formats that will fit your schedule better than the traditional fall and spring semesters. While it is pretty standard to have twelve to fifteen hours of classroom time per semester credit hour, classes vary in format. Some schools offer short summer sessions, winter terms, nine-week formats, and even concentrated classes during spring break. Many adult-format classes are offered one day a week so that there is less commuting time involved. Whenever classes meet, remember to bring a pillow! Those straight-backed chairs can be hard to sit in for three or more hours at a time!
- What hours does the school provide student services? If you are looking at a library where everything closes at 9 P.M. and a bookstore that closes at 5 P.M., it probably isn't an adult friendly campus.

How do you know you are an adult student?

There is no magic age that denotes an adult student, so the following list of indicators may help you tell whether or not you qualify. You know you are an adult student when:

- The class wants to use your clothes for a '50s drama.
- The teacher calls you sir.
- Your great-granddaughter tutors you on your homework.
- You use Poli-Grip to glue your leaf collection together.
- Your boyfriend takes you out for a wild night of warm milk and bingo.
- You can't remember which course you are taking after the class break.
- *You* are the history project.

If three or more of these indicators apply, you are officially an adult student.

Summary

Age and the knowledge that comes with it can be an advantage in the right educational program. Using the knowledge you have from life and work experience can be converted into valuable academic credits in accredited programs. Returning adults generally do better in school the second time around, which should help reduce the all-too-common anxiety around returning to school. The biggest enemy for most adults is not time or money, but fear of failure. This is usually overcome, though, after taking a course or two. The good news is that it's not too late to begin working toward your degree. You can still fulfill your dream.

APPENDIX A

Financial Aid Resources

Many books and brochures are written on the topic of financial aid. Listed below are some sources that may be of help in your research.

The Advisor: A Counselor's Guide to Student Financial Assistance. Washington, D.C.: National Association of Student Financial Aid Administrators, 1997. Approximate cost: $25. To order: NASFAA, Attn: Publications Desk, 1920 L St., NW, Suite 200, Department Web796ADV, Washington, DC 20036-5020.

"Applying for Financial Aid: A Guide for Parents and Students," 1994–95 edition. Iowa City, Iowa: American College Testing Program, 1993. Free. To order: Call 319-337-1410 or write to ACT, P.O. Box 168, Iowa City, IA 52243.

Astor, Bart. *You Can Afford College: The Family Guide to Meeting College Costs.* New York: Kaplan, 1995. Approximate cost: $15. To order: Bantam Doubleday Dell Publishers, 1540 Broadway, New York, NY 10036.

Bear, John B., and Mariah P. Bear. *Bear's Guide to Finding Money for College, 1996.* Berkeley, Calif.: Ten Speed Press, 1995. Approximate cost: $9.95. To order: Ten Speed Press, P.O. Box 7123, Berkeley, CA 94707.

Bellantoni, Patrick L. *College Financial Aid Made Easy.* 2d ed. Atlanta, Ga.: Tara Publishing, 1995. Approximate cost: $21. To order: Call 800-888-4741 or write to Independent Publishers Group, 814 North Franklin St., Chicago, IL 60610.

Black, Richard W. *The Complete Family Guide to College Financial Aid.* New York: Perigee Books, 1995. Approximate cost: $12. To order: Berkeley Publishing Group, 200 Madison Ave., New York, NY 10016.

Blum, Laurie. *Free Money from Colleges.* New York: Henry Holt, 1993. Approximate cost: $35. To order: Henry Holt and Company, 115 West 18th St., New York, NY 10011.

Cash for College. 1996–97 ed. Washington, D.C.: National Association of Student Financial Aid Administrators (NASFAA), 1996. Free. To order: http://www.nasfaa.org/public/cashfc.html

Cassidy, Daniel J. *The Scholarship Book.* 5th ed. Englewood Cliffs, N.J.: Prentice Hall, 1996. Approximate cost: $32.95.

Dennis, Marguerite J. *Complete College Financing Guide 1997.* Barron's Education Series. Hauppauge, N.Y.: Barron's, 1997. Approximate cost: $15. To order: Call 800-645-3476 or write to Barron's, 250 Wireless Blvd., Hauppauge, NY 11788.

Eisner, Elizabeth, and Valentina K. Tikoff. *Preparing Your Child for College: A Resource Book for Parents, 1996–97.* Washington, D.C.: U.S. Department of Education, 1996. Free. To order: Call 800-USA-LEARN or write to Catalog, Consumer Information Center, Pueblo, CO 81009.

Ferrara, Miranda H., and Sandra Jaszczak, *The Awards Almanac: An International Guide to Career, Research, and Education Funds, 1996.* Detroit: St. James Press, 1995. Approximate cost: $125. To order: St. James Press, 835 Penobscot Building, Detroit, MI 48226-4094.

Funding Your Education, 1996–97. Washington, D.C.: U.S. Department of Education, 1996. Free.

Hauptman, Arthur M. *The Tuition Dilemma: Assessing New Ways to Pay for College.* Washington, D.C.: Brookings Institution, 1990. Approximate cost: $8.95.

Krefetz, Gerald. *Paying for College: A Guide for Parents.* New York: College Board, 1995. Approximate cost: $14. To order: Call 800-323-7155 or write to College Board Publications, Box 886, New York, NY 10101-0886.

Leider, Anna, and Robert Leider. *Don't Miss Out: The Ambitious Student's Guide to Financial Aid.* 2d ed. Alexandria, Va.: Octameron

Associates, 1997. Approximate cost: $8.00. To order: Call 703-836-5480 or write to Octameron Associates, P.O. Box 2748, Alexandria, VA 22301.

Paying Less for College 1996. 13th ed. Princeton, N.J.: Peterson's Guides, 1995. Approximate cost: $26.95. To order: Call 800-EDU-DATA or write to Peterson's Guides, P.O. Box 2123, Princeton, NJ 08543-2123.

Timely Information for Parents and Students: Selecting and Paying for Your Education Beyond High School. 1996–97 ed. Washington, D.C.: National Association of Student Financial Aid Administrators, 1996. Approximate cost: $9. To order: NASFAA, 1920 L St., NW, Suite 200, Department TIPSWEB96, Washington, DC 20036-5020.

For a more comprehensive bibliography of more than 360 references for financial aid see the World Wide Web address http://www.finaid.org/finaid/bibliography/complete.html, which provides financial aid advice for students in specific gender, sports, state, and age categories.

APPENDIX B

Christian Colleges and Universities

This is a partial list of colleges that can be considered Christian. The list is intended to be a starting point for a college search, not an endorsement of specific colleges. The process for finding a school mentioned in the previous chapters should be used to research the schools mentioned below before any final decision is made.

Abilene Christian University
ACU Box 29100
Abilene, TX 79699-9100
Switchboard: 915-674-2000
Fax: 915-674-2958
Web site: http://www.acu.edu

Anderson University
1100 East Fifth St.
Anderson, IN 46012-3495
Switchboard: 317-649-9071
Fax: 317-641-3851
Web site: http://www.anderson.edu

Asbury College
1 Macklem Dr.
Wilmore, KY 40390-1198
Switchboard: 606-858-3511
Fax: 606-858-3921
Web site: http://www.asbury.edu

Atlantic Baptist University
333 Gorge Rd.
Moncton, New Brunswick E1C 8K2
CANADA
Switchboard: 506-858-8970
Fax: 506-858-9694
Web site: http://www.abu.nb.ca

Azusa Pacific University
P.O. Box 7000
901 East Alosta Ave.
Azusa, CA 91702-7000
Switchboard: 818-969-3434
Fax: 818-969-7180
Web site: http://www.apu.edu

Bartlesville Wesleyan College
2201 Silver Lake Rd.
Bartlesville, OK 74006-6299
Switchboard: 918-333-6151
Fax: 918-335-6210
Web site: http://www.bwc.edu

Belhaven College
1500 Peachtree St.
Jackson, MS 39202-1789
Switchboard: 601-968-5919
Fax: 601-968-9998
Web site: http://www.belhaven.edu

Bethel College (Indiana)
1001 West McKinley Ave.
Mishawaka, IN 46545
Switchboard: 219-259-8511
Fax: 219-257-3326
Web site: http://www.bethel-in.edu

Bethel College (Kansas)
300 East 27th St.
North Newton, KS 67117-9989
Switchboard: 316-283-2500
Fax: 316-284-5286
Web site: http://www.bethelks.edu

Bethel College (Minnesota)
3900 Bethel Dr.
St. Paul, MN 55112-6999
Switchboard: 612-638-6400
Fax: 612-638-6001
Web site: http://www.bethel.edu

Biola University
13800 Biola Ave.
La Mirada, CA 90639-0001
Switchboard: 310-903-6000
Fax: 310-903-4748
Web site: http://www.biola.edu

Bluffton College
280 West College Ave.
Bluffton, OH 45817-1196
Switchboard: 419-358-3000
Fax: 419-358-3323
Web site: http://www.bluffton.edu

Bryan College
P.O. Box 7000
Dayton, TN 37321-7000
Switchboard: 423-775-2041
Fax: 423-775-7330
Web site: http://www.bryan.edu

California Baptist College
8432 Magnolia Ave.
Riverside, CA 92504-3297
Switchboard: 909-689-5771
Fax: 909-351-1808
Web site: http://www.calbaptist.edu

Calvin College
3201 Burton St. SE
Grand Rapids, MI 49546
Switchboard: 616-957-6000
Fax: 616-957-8551
Web site: http://www.calvin.edu

Campbell University
215 Main St.
Buies Creek, NC 27506
Switchboard: 910-893-1200
Fax: 910-893-1424
Web site: http://www.campbell.edu

Campbellsville University
1 University Dr.
Campbellsville, KY 42718-2799
Switchboard: 502-789-5000 or 800-264-6014
Fax: 502-789-5050
Web site: http://www.campbellsvil.edu

Cedarville College
P.O. Box 601
251 N. Main St.
Cedarville, OH 45314-0601
Switchboard: 513-766-2211
Fax: 513-766-2760
Web site: http://www.cedarville.edu

Central Baptist College
1501 College Ave.
Conway, AR 72032
Switchboard: 501-329-6872
Fax: 501-329-2941

College of the Ozarks
Point Lookout, MO 65726
Switchboard: 417-334-6411
Fax: 417-335-2618
Web site: http://www.CofO.edu

Colorado Christian University
180 South Garrison St.
Lakewood, CO 80226
Switchboard: 303-202-0100
Fax: 303-274-7560 or 303-239-6380
Web site: http://www.ccu.edu

Cornerstone College
1001 E. Beltline Ave. NE
Grand Rapids, MI 49505-5897
Switchboard: 616-949-5300
Fax: 616-949-0875
Web site: http://www.cornerstone.edu

Covenant College
14049 Scenic Highway
Lookout Mountain, GA 30750
Switchboard: 706-820-1560
Fax: 706-820-2165
Web site: http://www.covenant.edu

Crichton College
P.O. Box 757830
6655 Winchester Rd.
Memphis, TN 38715-7830
Switchboard: 901-367-9800
Fax: 901-367-3866

The Criswell College
4010 Gaston Ave.
Dallas, TX 75264
Switchboard: 214-821-5433
Fax: 214-818-1310
Web site: http://www.criswell.edu

Dallas Baptist University
3000 Mountain Creek Parkway
Dallas, TX 75211-9299
Switchboard: 214-333-7100
Fax: 214-333-5115
Web site: http://www.dbu.edu

Dordt College
498 4th Ave. NE
Sioux Center, IA 51250-1697
Switchboard: 712-722-3771
Fax: 712-722-1198
Web site: http://www.dordt.edu

East Texas Baptist University
1209 North Grove
Marshall, TX 75670-1498
Switchboard: 903-935-7963
Fax: 903-938-1705
Web site: http://www.etbu.edu

Eastern College
10 Fairview Dr.
St. Davids, PA 19087-3696
Switchboard: 610-341-5800
Fax: 610-341-1375
Web site: http://www.eastern.edu

Eastern Mennonite University
1200 Park Rd.
Harrisonburg, VA 22801-2462
Switchboard: 540-432-4000
Fax: 540-432-4444
Web site: http://www.emu.edu

Eastern Nazarene College
23 E. Elm Ave.
Quincy, MA 02170-2999
Switchboard: 617-745-3000
Fax: 617-745-3590
Web site: http://www.enc.edu

Erskine College
2 Washington St.
Due West, SC 29639
Switchboard: 864-379-2131
Fax: 864-379-2167
Web site: http://www.erskine.edu

Evangel College
1111 North Glenstone
Springfield, MO 65802-2191
Switchboard: 417-865-2811
Fax: 417-865-9599
Web site: http://www.evangel.edu

Fresno Pacific University
1717 South Chestnut Ave.
Fresno, CA 93702
Switchboard: 209-453-2000
Fax: 209-453-2007
Web site: http://www.fresno.edu

Geneva College
3200 College Ave.
Beaver Falls, PA 15010-3599
Switchboard: 412-846-5100
Fax: 412-847-6687
Web site: http://www.geneva.edu

George Fox University
414 North Meridian St.
Newberg, OR 97132-2697
Switchboard: 503-538-8383
Fax: 503-537-3834
Web site: http://www.georgefox.edu

Gordon College
255 Grapevine Rd.
Wenham, MA 01984-1899
Switchboard: 508-927-2300
Fax: 508-524-3704
Web site: http://www.gordonc.edu

Goshen College
1700 South Main St.
Goshen, IN 46526-4794
Switchboard: 219-535-7000
Fax: 219-535-7660
Web site: http://www.goshen.edu

Grace College
200 Seminary Dr.
Winona Lake, IN 46590
Switchboard: 219-372-5100
Fax: 219-372-5265
Web site: http://www.grace.edu

Grand Canyon University
P.O. Box 11097
Phoenix, AZ 85061-1097
Switchboard: 602-249-3300
Fax: 602-589-2895
Web site: http://www.grand-canyon.edu

Greenville College
P.O. Box 159
Greenville, IL 62246-0159
Switchboard: 618-664-2800
Fax: 618-664-1748
Web site: http://www.greenville.edu

Hardin-Simmons University
P.O. Box 16000
Abeline, TX 79698-6000
Switchboard: 915-670-1206
Fax: 915-671-2115
Web site: http://www.hsutx.edu

Hope International University
(formerly Pacific Christian College)
2500 E. Nutwood Ave.
Fullerton, CA 92831
Switchboard: 714-879-3901
Fax: 714-526-0231
Web site: http://www.pacificcc.edu

Houghton College
1 Willard Ave.
Houghton, NY 14744
Switchboard: 716-567-9200
Fax: 716-567-9570
Web site: http://www.houghton.edu

Howard Payne University
1000 Fisk Ave.
Brownwood, TX 76801
Switchboard: 915-649-8030
Web site: http://www.hputx.edu

Huntington College
2303 College Ave.
Huntington, IN 46750
Switchboard: 219-356-6000 or 800-642-6493
Fax: 219-356-9448
Web site: http://www.huntington.edu

Indiana Wesleyan University
4201 South Washington
Marion, IN 46953
Switchboard: 317-674-6901
Fax: 317-677-2499
Web site: http://www.indwes.edu

International Christian University
Rennweg 1
A–1030 Vienna
AUSTRIA
Phone: (011-431) 718-50-6811
Fax: (011-431) 718-50-689
Web site: http://www.bcpl.lib.md.us/
~mdreimil/icu.html

John Brown University
2000 West University
Siloam Springs, AR 72761-2121
Switchboard: 501-524-9500
Fax: 501-524-9548
Web site: http://www.jbu.edu

Judson College
1151 North State St.
Elgin, IL 60123-1498
Switchboard: 847-695-2500
Fax: 847-695-0712
Web site: http://www.judson-il.edu

King College
1350 King College Rd.
Bristol, TN 37620
Switchboard: 423-968-1187
Fax: 423-968-4456
Web site: http://www.king.edu

The King's University College
9125—50 St.
Edmonton, Alberta T6B 2H3
CANADA
Switchboard: 403-465-3500
Fax: 403-465-3534
Web site: http://www.kingsu.ab.ca

Lee University
P.O. Box 3450
Cleveland, TN 37320-3450
1120 North Ocoee St.
Cleveland, TN 37311
Switchboard: 423-614-8000
Fax: 423-614-8016
Web site: http://www.leecollege.edu

LeTourneau University
P.O. Box 7001
Longview, TX 75607-7001
2100 South Mobberly
Longview, TX 75602
Switchboard: 903-233-3000
Fax: 903-233-3105 (president's office)
Web site: http://www.letu.edu

Malone College
515 25th St. NW
Canton, OH 44709-3897
Switchboard: 330-471-8100
Fax: 330-454-6977
Web site: http://www.malone.edu

The Master's College
21726 Placerita Canyon Rd.
Santa Clarita, CA 91321-1200
Switchboard: 805-259-3540
Fax: 805-254-1998
Web site: http://www.masters.edu

Messiah College
College Ave.
Grantham, PA 17027
Switchboard: 717-766-2511
Fax: 717-691-6025
Web site: http://www.messiah.edu

MidAmerica Nazarene College
2030 East College Way
Olathe, KS 66062-1899
Switchboard: 913-782-3750
Fax: 913-791-3290
Web site: http://www.mvnc.edu

Milligan College
Milligan College, TN 37682
Switchboard: 423-461-8700
Fax: 423-461-8755
Web site: http://www.milligan.edu

Montreat College
P.O. Box 1267
Montreat, NC 28757
Switchboard: 704-669-8012
Fax: 704-669-9554
Web site: http://www.montreat.edu

Mount Vernon Nazarene College
800 Martinsburg Rd.
Mount Vernon, OH 43050-9500
Switchboard: 614-397-1244
Fax: 614-397-2769
Web site: http://www.mvnc.edu

North Park University
3225 West Foster Ave.
Chicago, IL 60625-4895
Switchboard: 773-244-6200
Fax: 773-583-0858
Web site: http://www.northpark.edu

Northwest Christian College
828 East 11th Ave.
Eugene, OR 97401-3727
Switchboard: 541-343-1641
Fax: 541-343-9159
Web site: www.nwcc.edu

Northwest College
P.O. Box 579
Kirkland, WA 98083-0579
Switchboard: 206-822-8266
Fax: 206-827-0148
Web site: http://www.nwcollege.edu

Northwest Nazarene College
623 Holly St.
Nampa, ID 83686
Switchboard: 208-467-8011
Fax: 208-467-1098
Web site: http://www.nnc.edu

Northwestern College (Iowa)
101 Seventh St. SW
Orange City, IA 51041-1996
Switchboard: 712-737-7100
Fax: 712-737-7247
Web site: http://www.nwciowa.edu

Northwestern College (Minnesota)
3003 Snelling Ave.
Saint Paul, MN 55113-1598
Switchboard: 612-631-5100
Fax: 612-631-5269
Web site: http://www.nwc.edu

Nyack College
1 South Blvd.
Nyack, NY 10960-3698
Switchboard: 914-358-1710
Fax: 914-363-6429
Web site: http://www.nyackcollege.edu

Oklahoma Baptist University
500 West University
Shawnee, OK 74801-2590
Switchboard: 405-275-2850
Fax: 405-878-2069
Web site: http://www.okbu.edu

Oklahoma Christian
2501 E. Memorial Rd.
P.O. Box 11000
Oklahoma City, OK 73138-1100
Switchboard: 800-877-5010
Web site: http://www.oc.edu

Olivet Nazarene University
P.O. Box 592
Kankakee, IL 60901-0592
Switchboard: 815-939-5011
Fax: 815-935-4990
Web site: http://www.olivet.edu

Oral Roberts University
7777 South Lewis Ave.
Tulsa, OK 74171
Switchboard: 918-495-6161
Fax: 918-495-6033
Web site: http://www.oru.edu

Palm Beach Atlantic College
P.O. Box 24708
West Palm Beach, FL 33416-4708
Switchboard: 561-803-2000
Fax: 561-803-2186
Web site: http://www.pbac.edu

Philadelphia College of Bible
200 Manor Ave.
Langhorne, PA 19047-2990
Switchboard: 215-752-5800
Fax: 215-702-4341
Web site: http://www.pcb.edu

Point Loma Nazarene College
3900 Lomaland Dr.
San Diego, CA 92106-2899
Switchboard: 619-849-2200
Fax: 619-849-2579
Web site: http://www.ptloma.edu

Providence College and Seminary
Otterburne, Manitoba R0A 1G0
CANADA
Switchboard: 204-433-7488
Fax: 204-433-7158
Web site: http://www.providence.mb.ca

Redeemer College
777 Highway 53 East
Ancaster, Ontario L9K 1J4
CANADA
Switchboard: 905-648-2131
Fax: 905-648-2134
Web site: http://www.redeemer.on.ca

Roberts Wesleyan College
2301 Westside Dr.
Rochester, NY 14624-1997
Switchboard: 716-594-6000
Fax: 716-594-6371
Web site: http://www.roberts.edu

Seattle Pacific University
3307 Third Ave. West
Seattle, WA 98119
Switchboard: 206-281-2000
Fax: 206-281-2500
Web site: http://www.spu.edu

Simpson College
2211 College View Dr.
Redding, CA 96003-8606
Switchboard: 916-224-5600
Fax: 916-224-5608
Web site: http://www.simpsonca.edu

Southern California College
55 Fair Dr.
Costa Mesa, CA 92626
Switchboard: 714-556-3610
Fax: 714-957-9317
Web site: http://www.sccu.edu

Southern Nazarene University
6729 NW 39th Expressway
Bethany, OK 73008
Switchboard: 405-789-6400
Fax: 405-491-6381
Web site: http://www.snu.edu

Southern Wesleyan University
P.O. Box 1020
Central, SC 29630-1020
Switchboard: 864-639-2453
Fax: 864-639-0826
Web site: http://www.swu.edu

Southwest Baptist University
1600 University Ave.
Bolivar, MO 65613
Switchboard: 417-326-5281
Fax: 417-326-1514
Web site: http://www.sbuniv.edu

Spring Arbor College
Spring Arbor, MI 49283
Switchboard: 517-750-1200
Fax: 517-750-2108
Web site: http://www.arbor.edu

Sterling College
Sterling, KS 67579
Switchboard: 316-278-2173
Fax: 316-278-3188
Web site: http://www.sterling.edu

Tabor College
400 South Jefferson
Hillsboro, KS 67063-1799
Switchboard: 316-947-3121
Fax: 316-947-2607
Web site: http://www.tabor.edu

Taylor University
500 W. Reade Ave.
Upland, IN 46989-1001
Switchboard: 317-998-2751
Fax: 317-998-5569
Web site: http://www.tayloru.edu

Trevecca Nazarene University
333 Murfreesboro Rd.
Nashville, TN 37210-2877
Switchboard: 615-248-1200
Fax: 615-248-7728
Web site: http://www.trevecca.edu

Trinity Christian College
6601 West College Dr.
Palos Heights, IL 60463-0929
Switchboard: 708-597-3000
Fax: 708-385-5665
Web site: http://www.trnty.edu

Trinity International University
College of Arts and Sciences
2065 Half Day Rd.
Deerfield, IL 60015
Switchboard: 847-945-8800
Fax: 847-317-8090
Web site: http://www.tiu.edu

Trinity International University
South Florida Campus
P.O. Box 019674
Miami, FL 33101
Phone: 305-577-4600
Fax: 305-577-4612

Trinity Western University
7600 Glover Rd.
Langly, British Columbia V2Y 1Y1
CANADA
Switchboard: 604-888-7511
Fax: 604-888-5336
Web site: http://www.twu.ca
U.S. mailing address:
P.O. Box 1409
Blaine, WA 98231-1409

Union University
2447 Highway 45 Bypass
Jackson, TN 38305-3697
Switchboard: 901-668-1818
Fax: 901-661-5175
Web site: http://www.uu.edu

University of Mary Hardin-Baylor
Box 8001, UMHB Station
Belton, TX 76513
Switchboard: 254-939-4590
Fax: 254-939-4535
Web site: http://www.umhb.edu

University of Sioux Falls
1101 West 22nd St.
Sioux Falls, SD 57105-1699
Switchboard: 605-331-5000
Fax: 605-331-6615
Web site: http://www.thecoo.edu

Warner Pacific College
2219 SE 68th Ave.
Portland, OR 97215-4099
Switchboard: 503-775-4366
Fax: 503-775-8853
Web site: http://www.warnerpacific.edu

Warner Southern College
5301 US Highway 27 South
Lake Wales, FL 33853
Switchboard: 941-638-1426
Fax: 941-638-1472
Web site: http://www.warner.edu

Wayland Baptist University
1900 West Seventh
Plainview, TX 79072-6998
Switchboard: 806-296-5521
Web site: http://www.wbu.edu

Western Baptist College
5000 Deer Park Dr. SE
Salem, OR 97301
Switchboard: 503-581-8600
Fax: 503-585-4316
Web site: http://www.wbc.edu

Westmont College
955 La Paz Rd.
Santa Barbara, CA 93108-1099
Switchboard: 805-565-6000
Fax: 805-565-6234
Web site: http://www.westmont.edu

Wheaton College
501 College Ave.
Wheaton, IL 60187-5593
Switchboard: 630-752-5000
Fax: 630-752-5555
Web site: http://www.wheaton.edu

Whitworth College
300 West Hawthorne Rd.
Spokane, WA 99251
Switchboard: 509-466-1000
Fax: 509-466-3773
Web site: http://www.whitworth.edu

William Tyndale College
37500 West Twelve Mile Rd.
Farmington Hills, MI 48331-3147
Switchboard: 810-553-7200
Fax: 810-553-5963

Williams Baptist College
201 Fulbright Ave.
Walnut Ridge, AR 72476
Switchboard: 501-886-6741
Fax: 501-886-3924
Web site: http://wb2.wbcoll.edu

APPENDIX C

Web Pages by Denomination

**http://www.yahoo.com/Society_and_Culture/Religion/
Christianity/Education/Colleges_and_Universities/**
More web pages that list colleges by denomination can be found
at the Internet address above for the following church groups:

Anglican

Assemblies of God

Baptist

Catholic

Christian Reformed Church

Church of Christ

Church of the Brethren

Church of the Nazarene

Disciples of Christ

Evangelical Lutheran Church
in America

Fellowship of Grace Brethren

Free Methodist

Lutheran

Mennonite

Moravian Church

Pentecostal

Presbyterian

Reformed Church in
America

Seventh-day Adventists

Society of Friends

United Church of Christ

United Methodist Church

Notes

Chapter 1 *Eenie, Meenie, Miney, Moe*

1. "Of Questionable Worth," *The Dallas Morning News,* 28 January 1997, sec., p. 16A.

2. Ibid., 17A.

Chapter 2 *We're Not in Kansas Anymore, Toto!*

1. Dinesh D'Souza, *Illiberal Education: The Politics of Race and Sex on Campus* (New York: Vintage Books, 1992), 9–10.

2. George M. Marsden, *The Soul of the American University* (New York: Oxford Press, 1994), 11.

3. D'Souza, *Illiberal Education,* 12.

4. Thomas Sowell, *Choosing a College: A Guide for Parents and Students* (New York: Harper and Row, 1989), 4.

5. David A. Hoekema, *Campus Rules and Moral Community: In Place of In Loco Parentis* (Lanham, Md.: Rowman & Littlefield Publishers, 1994), 55.

6. Ibid.

Chapter 3 *Can I Really Afford It?*

1. "Finances Are Becoming More Crucial in Students' College Choice, Survey Finds," *The Chronicle of Higher Education,* 17 January 1997, sec. A., p. 41.

2. "The American Freshman: National Norms for 1996" (Los Angeles: American Council on Education and UCLA Higher Education Research Institute, 1996).

3. Karen Heller and Lily Eng, "Academia's Greek Tycoon," *Reader's Digest* (October 1996), 128.

4. *The News, Coalition for Christian Colleges and Universities* (January/February 1997), 1.

5. Jane Noble Suhler, "College Debts Smaller than People Think," *Dallas Morning News,* 16 May 1997, 1.

6. Ibid., sec. A, p. 14.

7. Internet site: http://www.ucop.edu/ucophome/budget/uclafee.html (8 April 1997).

8. Suhler, "College Debts Smaller," 1.

9. "Finances Are Becoming More Crucial," sec. A, p. 41.

Chapter 4 *A Key to Your College Education*

1. Kelly McCollum, "One Way to Get into College: Buy an Essay That Worked for Someone Else," *The Chronicle of Higher Education,* 28 February 1997, sec. A, p. 25.

Chapter 7 *A Match Made in Heaven*

1. Sheri Drais, "Place of Worship," *APU* (Azusa Pacific University) *Life* (Winter 1997), 6.
2. *Choose a Christian College* (Petersons Guides).

Chapter 8 *When a Secular University Is the Best Choice*

1. http://www.gospelcom.net/iv/general/vision.html.
2. http://www.gospelcom.net/navs/.
3. http://www.cci.org/campus-ministry.
4. http://www.bgct.org/.

Chapter 9 *College Accreditation*

1. "FBI Agents Raid Correspondence School," the *Chronicle of Higher Education,* 26 July 1996, A4.

Chapter 10 *Excuuuuuse Me!*

1. "The American Freshman,".
2. Ed Hollinger, "How Faith Fits into Your College Search," *Campus Life* (October 1996), 98.
3. Ibid., 98.
4. Julie Adams and James Keeley, "The Samaritan Within," Psychology 4319 Research Methods Class, Dallas Baptist University, 8 April 1997.

Chapter 11 *The First Six Weeks of College*

1. Jay L. Kesler, *Challenges for the College Bound* (Grand Rapids: Baker, 1994), 72.
2. David Early, "The Early Zone: Stoopid Roommate Tricks," *Campus Life* (Special Issue, February 1997), 54–55.
3. Joe Urschel, "How Girls Get Scared Away from Computers," *USA Today,* 26 June 1996, sec. D, 1.
4. Ibid., 2.

Chapter 12 *The Parent of a New College Student*

1. "America's Best Colleges," *US News and World Report,* 1997, 30.
2. Family Policy and Regulations Office, Department of Education, Washington, D.C. 20202.
3. "America's Best Colleges," 37.

Chapter 14 *The Challenge of Changing Schools*

1. "Transfer Behavior among Beginning Postsecondary Students: 1989–94," National Center for Educational Statistics. Internet site: http://www.ed.gov./NCES/pubs97/97266 .html (2 June 1997), 1.
2. "Top 153 Signs You've Been in College Too Long," *Keeper of the Lists,* Internet site: www.dtd.com (17 February 1997).
3. Dan Corrigan, *The Internet University* (Harwich, Mass.: Cape Software Press, 1996), 78.
4. Jennifer Wilcha and David A. Smith, *The College Student's Guide to Transferring Schools* (New York: Avion Books, 1990), 68.

Chapter 15 *Distance Learning*

1. Kevin Maney, "Technology Is 'Demolishing' Time, Distance," *USA Today,* 24 April 1997, sec. B, p. 2.
2. Jim Hughes, http://ucinix.san.uc.edu/~hughesj/wright/wright.html.
3. http://members.aol.com/jwbriggs/blueax/index.html.
4. http://www.ionet.net/~jellenc/ae_intro.html.
5. http://www.wpafb.af.mil/museum.
6. Dawn Kuczwara, http://www.tezcat .com/~dawn/warplane/warplane.html.

Chapter 16 *Okay, So I'm an Adult Who Wants a Degree*

1. Jean Nash Johnson, "Studies in Determination," *Dallas Morning News,* 25 May 1997, sec. F, pp. 1–4.

Dr. Larry Linamen is provost and academic vice president of graduate programs for Dallas Baptist University. He has twenty years experience in higher education, having served at five different universities, ranging from large public institutions to small private Christian universities. In 1988 he spent six months teaching in Communist China as a foreign expert at Lanzhou Commercial College in Gansu Province.

Formerly vice president of the Barna Research Group, Dr. Linamen is a recipient of the Valley Forge Foundation's George Washington Medal for excellence in teaching from the Valley Forge Foundation, has been named to the Texas Hall of Fame, and is a member of Who's Who Among America's Teachers. He holds a doctorate in education and MBA from Ball State University and a bachelor of science in accounting and business administration from Anderson University.

He lives in Duncanville, Texas, with his wife, Karen, and daughters Kaitlyn and Kacie.